BIG-TIME BASEBALL is a record of major league proceedings between 1900 and 1978. Here is an array of all the colorful personalities, thrilling episodes, records, famous players, blunders, hilarious humor, and big moments that have endeared baseball to the hearts of millions.

Even though you have been an ardent baseball fan for years, you will find much in this book that you didn't know—unusual records, fascinating anecdotes, and rare pictures.

BIG-TIME BASEBALL contains complete pitching and batting records, World Series winners, and all the other data that would interest any baseball fan.

BIG-TIME BASEBALL

A Complete Record of the National Sport

Maury Allen

HART PUBLISHING COMPANY, INC. • NEW YORK CITY

THIS BOOK IS DEDICATED TO
IKE GELLIS
A BOSS, A FRIEND, AND A TEACHER

COPYRIGHT © 1978 HART PUBLISHING COMPANY, INC.
NEW YORK, NEW YORK 10003

ISBN NO. 08055-0400-1
LIBRARY OF CONGRESS CATALOG NO. 78-71349

MANUFACTURED IN THE UNITED STATES OF AMERICA

CONTENTS

THE ALL-STAR TEAM OF ALL TIME

Every true baseball fan has enjoyed the pleasant daydream in which the great players of all time take the field together. Though Baseball's Hall of Fame at Cooperstown has named its individual immortals, no official board has ever selected an all-star aggregation.

Disregarding criticism and consequence, a selection committee was nominated to choose an all-time, all-star baseball team. This committee numbered among it members 92 topflight sportswriters of the country's leading newspapers, as well as 44 nationally-known public figures.

Every baseball fan will want to become acquainted with the stories of these all-time greats, whose skill and daring on the ballfield has been the stuff of which legends are made. These players truly carried the game to the summit of popularity and national acclaim it enjoys today.

Turn the page and see the men the top sports scribes and noted baseball fans have picked for the All-Star Team of All Time.

THE SELECTORS OF THE ALL-STAR TEAM OF ALL TIME

The following names compose the panel who chose the four All-Star Teams set forth in this book. These men constitute a roster of baseball's cognoscenti. They have all been associated with the game for many, many years. If anybody knows baseball, it is they.

Our thanks to them for their participation in this effort.

Bowie Kuhn	*Commissioner of Baseball*	Arthur Richman	*New York Mets*
Bob Wirz	*Director of Information*	Tim Hamilton	*New York Mets*
Art Berke	*Asst. Dir. of Information*	Whitney de Roulet	*New York Mets*
Monte Irvin	*Asst. Dir. of Information*	Larry Shenk	*Philadelphia Phillies*
Ken Smith	*Baseball Hall of Fame*	Bill Guilfoile	*Pittsburgh Pirates*
Seymour Siwoff	*Statistician*	Jim Toomey	*St. Louis Cardinals*
Lee MacPhail	*President, American League*	Bob Chandler	*San Diego Padres*
Bob Fishel	*Asst. to Pres., American League*	Stu Smith	*San Francisco Giants*
Charles Feeney	*President, National League*	Marty Appel	*New York Yankees*
Blake Cullen	*PR Director, National League*	Buck Peden	*Chicago Cubs*
Bob Brown	*Baltimore Orioles*	Steve Brener	*Los Angeles Dodgers*
Bill Crowley	*Boston Red Sox*	Paul Durkin	*New York Daily News*
Tom Seeberg	*California Angels*	Moss Klein	*Newark Star Ledger*
Don Unferth	*Chicago White Sox*	Jack Lindberg	*Kansas City Star*
Joe Bick	*Cleveland Indians*	Will Grimsley	*The Associated Press*
Hal Middlesworth	*Detroit Tigers*	Sandy Oppenheimer	*Levittown Times*
Dean Vogelaar	*Kansas City Royals*	Don Seeholzer	*Painesville Telegraph*
Tom Skibosh	*Milwaukee Brewers*	Ed Browalski	*Detroit Polish Daily News*
Tom Mee	*Minnesota Twins*	Jim Vipond	*Toronto Globe and Mail*
Mickey Morabito	*New York Yankees*	Fred Turner	*The Patriot Ledger*
Larry Wahl	*New York Yankees*	Hal Snyder	*Santa Ana Register*
Carl Finley	*Oakland A's*	Rick Sayers	*Boston Herald American*
Randy Adamack	*Seattle Mariners*	Murray Rose	*The Associated Press*
Burt Hawkins	*Texas Rangers*	Vince Doria	*Boston Globe*
Howard Starkman	*Toronto Blue Jays*	Ted Diadinn	*Willoughby News Herald*
Bob Hope	*Atlanta Braves*	John Buckley	*Worcester Gazette*
Jim Ferguson	*Cincinnati Reds*	Paul Zimmerman	*New York Post*
Art Perkins	*Houston Astros*	Pat Livingston	*Pittsburgh Press*
Rodger Brulotte	*Montreal Expos*	Hugh McCovern	*Worcester Telegram*

Al Ames	*Glendale News Press*	Jim Rhode	*San Gabriel Times*
Bob Dolgan	*Cleveland Plain Dealer*	Red Smith	*New York Times*
Gene Legeza	*Lorain Journal*	Joe Gergen	*Newsday*
Larry Tarleton	*Dallas Times Herald*	Ron Swoboda	*CBS-TV*
Carl Peterson	*St. Paul Pioneer Press*	Bill Mazer	*WNEW-TV*
Jack Lang	*New York Daily News*	Ray Sons	*Chicago Sun-Times*
Joe Donnelly	*Newsday*	Hal Lebovitz	*Cleveland Plain Dealer*
Phil Pepe	*New York Daily News*	Bob August	*Cleveland Press*
Dan Stoneking	*Minneapolis Star*	Bob Stewart	*Canton Repository*
Bernie Kennedy	*Mt. Clemens Macomb Daily*	Herb Boldt	*Detroit News*
Scoop Lewis	*Bucks Country Courier Times*	Dick Mackey	*Kansas City Times*
Sal Marchiano	*WABC-TV*	Bud Lea	*Milwaukee Journal*
Jerome Holtzman	*Chicago Sun Times*	Arno Goethal	*St. Paul Dispatch*
Joe McGuff	*Kansas City Star*	Harold Claassen	*New York Times*
Furman Bisher	*Atlanta Journal*	Dick Sadler	*Newsday*
Dave Anderson	*New York Times*	Wick Temple	*The Associated Press*
Chuck Perazich	*Youngstown Vindicator*	Milton Richman	*United Press International*
Michael Bogen	*Springfield Union*	Bob Valli	*Oakland Tribune*
John Owen	*Seattle Post Intelligencer*	George Wallace	*Fort Worth Star*
Bruce Jenkins	*San Francisco Chronicle*	Jim Montgomery	*Cincinnati Enquirer*
John Dixon	*Long Beach Independent*	Tom Tulley	*Cincinnati Post*
Rick Davis	*San Diego Tribune*	Red Fisher	*Montreal Star*
George Langford	*Chicago Tribune*	Jay Searcy	*Philadelphia Inquirer*
Doug Frambes	*Camden Courier-Post*	Mike Rathet	*Philadelphia Daily News*
Ladd Neuman	*Detroit Free Press*	Herb Stutz	*Philadelphia Bulletin*
Bill Shirley	*Los Angeles Times*	Stan Hochman	*Philadephia Daily News*
Don Sherlock	*Bergen Record*	Bill Fleishman	*St. Louis Globe Democrat*
Tom Melody	*Akron Beacon Journal*	Red Foley	*New York Daily News*
Willie Klein	*Newark Star Ledger*	Hal Bock	*The Associated Press*
Jesse Outlar	*Atlanta Constitution*	Bill Madden	*New York Daily News*
Gene Buonaccorsi	*Providence Journal*	Fred McMane	*United Press International*
Bus Saidt	*Trenton Times*	Bob Posen	*St. Louis Post Dispatch*
Bill Tanton	*Baltimore Sun*	Joe Stein	*San Diego Tribune*
Peter May	*United Press International*	Bob Maisel	*Baltimore Morning Sun*
Dick Schaap	*NBC-TV*	John Steadman	*Baltimore News American*
Dave Beronio	*Vallejo Independent Press*	Dave Smith	*Washington Star*
Bob Hentzen	*Topeka Capital Journal*	Morrie Seigel	*Washington Star*
Hy Zimmerman	*Seattle Times*	Red Hoffman	*Lynn Item*
Fred Meiers	*San Bernadino Telegram*	Jim Murray	*Los Angeles Times*

Willie Mays

Honus Wagner

Brooks Robinson

THE ALL-STAR TEAM
OF ALL TIME

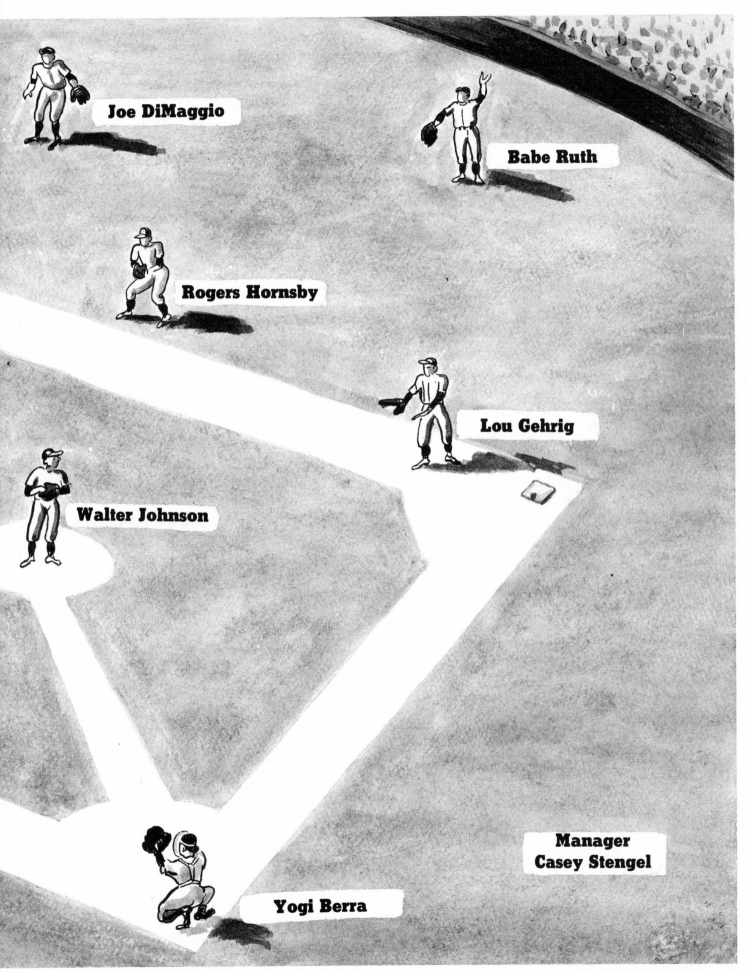

Joe DiMaggio

Babe Ruth

Rogers Hornsby

Lou Gehrig

Walter Johnson

Manager
Casey Stengel

Yogi Berra

NOTES ON THE SELECTIONS OF THE ALL-STAR TEAM OF ALL TIME

Baseball has been played professionally in this country for more than 100 years. There have been more than 10,000 players in organized baseball, less than 150 in the Baseball Hall of Fame, and more than two dozen players considered living legends of the Great American Pastime.

But to pick just nine players—*the best nine players ever*—seemed an insurmountable task. So I turned to the leading sportswriters who have covered baseball for years. We distributed close to 200 ballots and received 136 returns, a remarkable response.

For the All-Star team, the voters were given four choices for each position, except outfielders where they were given nine. Voters also had the privilege to write-in any candidate of their choice.

Voters were asked to select four All-Star teams in all. The first team was the All-Star Team of All Time. The other three were divided by era.

The battles were close; the voters were opinionated. Only Babe Ruth received all 136 votes—for outfield. DiMaggio received 111 votes, and Mays garnered 107.

The infield was more clear-cut. Lou Gehrig received 127 votes for first baseman. Rogers Hornsby received 97 votes for second baseman. Honus Wagner got 111 votes for shortstop, beating Joe Cronin. Brooks Robinson collected 54 votes for third baseman, just enough to edge out Pie Traynor who got 49 votes.

Yogi Berra ran surprisingly strong as catcher with 103 votes. Walter Johnson dominated the All-Time pitchers with 114.

Casey Stengel, John McGraw, and Joe McCarthy battled it out for the managerial post with Stengel winning with 49 votes. John McGraw came in second.

Warren Spahn, getting a great deal of support from younger voters, finished just behind Walter Johnson for pitcher. Micky Cochrane, the great catcher of the Tigers, finished second to Yogi Berra. Cochrane hit .320 and is considered by many the best defensive catcher the game has ever seen. Bill Terry, a .341 lifetime hitter—he batted .401 in 1930— trailed Lou Gehrig for first baseman. Jackie Robinson, the first Negro in Major League baseball and a lifetime .311 hitter, was runner-up for second baseman.

Some of the voters were up a tree. Bill Shirley, of the *Los Angeles Times* couldn't pick three outfielders and had to settle on five. He nominated Aaron, Cobb, DiMaggio, Mays, and Ruth. Bus Saidt of the *Trenton Times* expressed the same opinion by saying, "No way to keep Mantle and Mays off"—after he cast his ballots for DiMaggio, Ruth, and Williams. Bob Hope of the Atlanta Braves kept checking Hank Aaron's name every place he found it.

Paul Zimmerman of the *New York Post* went as far back as Cap Anson for his best manager. Steve Brener of the Los Angeles Dodgers didn't favor the nomination of Pete Rose as a third baseman. "He's an outfielder, not a third baseman," Brener said. Jim Toomey of the St. Louis Cardinals argued hard for St. Louis pitcher Bob Gibson.

Jack Lang of the *New York Daily News* pushed for old Dodger Roy Campanella. Dan Stoneking of the *Minneapolis Star* wrote, "I hope you don't toss out my write-in for Stan Musial." *New York Times* columnist Dave Anderson also plunked hard for Stan Musial. And who would disagree?

Atlanta Journal columnist, Furman Bisher was unhappy leaving off Hank Aaron in favor of his chosen outfield of Cobb, DiMaggio, and Ruth. Joe McGuff of the *Kansas City Star* changed his choice of Cobb; he erased him for Williams. On the other hand, Jerome Holtzman of the *Chicago Sun-Times* took Williams off his ballot in favor of Cobb. That's what makes a neck-and-neck horse race.

ABC television sportscaster Sal Marchiano was one of the few to almost match the consensus.

All in all, thanks fellows, for picking the best of the best. And now, on with the arguments.

THE RUNNERS-UP

Warren Spahn, *Pitcher*	**Hank Aaron,** *Outfielder*
Mickey Cochrane, *Catcher*	**Ted Williams,** *Outfielder*
Bill Terry, *First Baseman*	**Mickey Mantle,** *Outfielder*
Jackie Robinson, *Second Baseman*	**Stan Musial,** *Outfielder*
Joe Cronin, *Shortstop*	**Tris Speaker,** *Outfielder*
Pie Traynor, *Third Baseman*	**John McGraw,** *Manager*

WALTER JOHNSON

The king of pitchers.

For the most part, there wasn't anything tricky about Walter Johnson's delivery. He just threw a fastball. If that didn't work, he threw a faster one. The didn't give the batters much comfort but it did provide them with a ready-made alibi: "How can you hit 'em, if you can't see 'em?"

In one game, Ray Chapman facing Johnson, took two burning strikes. Then he stepped out of the batter's box and started back for the dugout. "Wait a minute," called the umpire, "you've got another strike coming." "Never mind," shrugged Chapman. "I don't want it."

That was Chapman's privilege, but Walter Johnson had no objection to giving batters their full allotment of three strikes. He just kept pouring them in, and batters just kept swinging. In his 21-year career, the Big Train dished out 3,508 sizzling strikeouts—a record that looks safe for all time. During that time, Johnson led the league for 12 years as the strikeout king.

In one game, it looked as though the Big Train was about to be derailed. The bases had suddenly filled with Red Sox on an error, a hit batter, and a base-on-balls—all charged to Johnson. To make things darker, there was no one out. Shortstop George McBride, then playing-manager of the Senators, called time and walked in to give Johnson a few well-meant words of advice.

"Now, now, George," Johnson chided gently. "Suppose you go back and play shortstop, and let me do the pitching."

The Big Train then opened the trottle and fanned Tris Speaker, Harry Hooper, and Duffy Lewis on nine straight pitches!

Sir Walter hung up a lifetime record of 113 shutout games.

For a period of over a month—from April 10th to May 14th, 1913—no one pushed across a single run against Johnson! When the bruised and desperate Browns finally managed to drive a tally across the plate in the fourth inning of a lopsided game on May 14th, they ended Johnson's staggering streak of 56 scoreless innings! No other hurler had ever come up with such a magnificent performance until Don Drysdale recorded 58 scoreless innings in 1968.

YOGI BERRA

Best in the clutch.

Yogi Berra was master of the malaprop. When he managed the Mets someone asked him what he thought of his team's pennant chances. "It ain't over till it's over," said Yogi. He was right. His Mets came from behind to win the 1973 pennant.

A squat, unattractive man off the field, Berra was probably the greatest clutch hitter the game has ever seen, a marvelous defensive catcher with a strong arm, an excellent outfielder in his later days, and a slugger of much renown. Berra batted often enough to collect 358 home runs in his long career with the Yankees from 1946 through 1963. He managed the Yanks to a pennant in 1964, then moved over to the Mets as a coach in 1965, under his old Yankee manager, Casey Stengel.

Lawrence Peter Berra was born in St. Louis on May 12, 1925. When his best friend, Joe Garagiola, signed a $500 bonus contract with the Cardinals, Berra wanted the same. He didn't get it, so he refused to sign with St. Louis.

The Yankees came along and offered him the $500. However, before he could join the team, World War II intervened and Berra was off to the Navy where he served with distinction.

Yogi returned late in 1946, caught and played the outfield in 1947, and became the regular Yankee catcher in 1948.

In 12 years under Casey Stengel, he played on 10 Yankee pennant winners, and played on three more under Ralph Houk. Berra managed the Yanks to the pennant in 1964. After losing the World Series in the seventh game to St. Louis, he was fired.

Yogi—named after a cartoon-movie character of an Indian yoga man—was named the American League's Most Valuable Player on three separate occasions. Famed as a bad-ball hitter, Yogi was able to hit any pitch any time if a base hit was vital. He was a strong, durable player who holds the record (313) for most home runs by a catcher. He was elected to the Hall of Fame in 1972.

After being let go as manager of the Mets in 1975, Berra returned to his first team, and has been a Yankee coach ever since.

LOU GEHRIG

Pride of the Yankees.

Early in May of 1925, Everett Scott, aging shortstop of the Yankees, stepped out from the lineup severing an almost incredible string of 1,307 consecutive games. Fans said no one would see the equal.

Less than a month later on June 1st, a 22-year-old youngster slipped almost unnoticed into the Yankee lineup. Sports scribes, searching for a nickname for the personable, shy youngster, harked back to his college days. They called him Columbia Lou—later to become Larrupin' Lou.

As the years rolled by, Gehrig became the Yanks' stalwart. He played in game after game and starred in game after game. Lou Gehrig never left the Yankee lineup even for a day, until May 2, 1939—14 years later. Larrupin' Lou had become The Iron Horse. Everett Scott's mark of 1,307 consecutive games was so far surpassed, it now seemed puny. Lou Gehrig wound up playing in 2,130 consecutive games.

As an extra-base hitter, Gehrig rivaled the great Bambino himself. He led the league in runs batted-in for 13 seasons—a mark which he shares with Ruth. For 14 years, he slugged out more than 100 extra-base hits a season—another record he shares with with The Babe.

In the home run department, Gehrig, of course, came off second to his mighty teammate, but by no means a bad second. Lou lambasted over 40 circuit drives during each of five seasons. In two of these, he hit 49—a handsome mark. Gehrig was the first man in baseball history who ever hit four consecutive home runs during a nine-inning game. He performed this prodigious feat on June 3, 1932. The baseball world gasped. You still find it hard to believe.

In 1931, Lou hit a homer in each of the six consecutive games. Three of these mighty blows cleared loaded bases. In his big-time career, Lou banged out 23 grand-slam home runs!

Lou Gehrig was a New Yorker from start to finish. His entire major league career was spent with the Yankees. And New York has given The Iron Horse a signal honor. Lou Gehrig was the first ballplayer to have a New York street named after him. Fans approaching Yankee Stadium now walk along Lou Gehrig Plaza.

ROGERS HORNSBY

The National League's greatest star.

"Get in closer to the plate! Choke up the bat! How do you expect to learn to hit that way?" Miller Huggins, manager of the 1915 Cardinals, was understandably exasperated. The new infielder, just up from the Denison Club of the Western Association, stubbornly shook his head. He kept his stance at the extreme outside corner of the batter's box. He kept his hands together at the end of the handle.

Miller Huggins never did make him change his batting style. "Oh, well," the manager sighed philosophically, "what kind of player can you expect to get for $400?"

Certainly not a league-leading batter. *But that's what Huggins got!* In fact, the Cards had obtained a slugger who was destined to lead the National League seven times. Yes, sir! Huggins had bought a .400 hitter for $400. Later, the Cardinals were to add a few zeros to that figure. In a few years, Hornsby was drawing down $40,000 a season.

Only two men in baseball history have ever hit .400 for three seasons: the immortal Ty Cobb and Hornsby. And the Rajah came within $3/10$ percent of reaching this mark a fourth time.

Hornsby holds the record for the highest batting average ever compiled during any one season. In 1924, the Rajah smote the pellet for a resounding .424. No one has beaten that record to date.

The Rajah was always aware of his destiny as a ballplayer, and treasured his magnificent pair of eyes. He avoided movies, reading on trains, and any strain that might lessen the precision of his wonderful timing.

It paid off. He was a terrific ballplayer on the field as well as with the stick. Although chiefly renowned today as a hitter, Rogers was a ball of fire who inspired his team to a pitch of fighting spirit. It was Manager Hornsby who led the Cardinals to their first pennant and to a victory over the Yankees in the World Series. But Hornsby's hitting was so spectacular that all his other achievements have more or less paled. For with a lifetime average of .358, the Rajah was the greatest hitter the National League has ever seen.

HONUS WAGNER

The bandylegged wonder.

A Giant rookie about to face the Pirates, once asked John McGraw how he should pitch to Honus Wagner. "Just throw the ball and pray," was McGraw's reply.

No cagier batter ever waved a stick at a pitcher than John Peter Wagner. He stood far away from the plate, at the extreme corner of the batter's box, and stepped into the pitch.

For 17 consecutive years, he batted over .300—winning the National League batting crown eight times—the best mark in League history.

But good as he was as a batsman, the Flying Dutchman was an in-fielder par excellence. They haven't come much better.

He wasn't much to look at, this Wagner. Just about medium height, solid and bandylegged—but all muscles. And hands so huge you couldn't always tell whether he was wearing his glove. His legs were so bowed you might roll a barrel through them. *But seldom a baseball!*

For Wagner possessed a virtuosity on the diamond that has rarely, if ever, been paralleled. He could come up with a throw from any position—crouching, kneeling, or on the dead-run. His peg, underhand or overhand, always traveled with bullet speed and rifle accuracy. Many a time he brought the crowds cheering to their feet by skipping nimbly into the short field behind third, and spearing a sizzler that had broken through the third baseman's mitts, and slipping it to first for the putout.

Honus studied the habits of players and seemed to sense just where the ball was going. When it arrived anywhere near shortstop, you could be sure that the Flying Dutchman would be right on top of it.

On the base paths, Honus was a greyhound. From a standing start on the far side of home plate, he once was clocked running the 30-plus yards to first base in $3\frac{2}{5}$ seconds.

A master of the stolen base, Wagner would bend his bandylegs into a slick slide. Time and again, the baffled baseman would reach down and tag nothing but dirt, only to find the Dutchman lying comfortably with his toe hooked securely around the sack.

BROOKS ROBINSON

The man with the magic glove.

In the 1970 World Series against the Cincinnati Reds, Brooks Robinson batted .429 and hardly anyone noticed. What was noticed was the amazing performance of Robinson on third base where he made more spectacular diving catches in one Series than most players make in a lifetime!

"He must have a magnet in there," said Cincinnati catcher Johnny Bench. "Every time we hit a ball, it seems to be drawn into that glove."

Not particularly fast on his feet, Robinson seemed to have the most incredible reflexes ever seen. He could dive for a ball, smother it, get to one knee and throw to first harder than most people can do while standing up.

It was Robinson who made baseball fans aware of the importance of defense to any successful team. While Robinson anchored third base, the Orioles dominated the American League for more than a decade.

At bat, Brooks was a long ball hitter who picked his spots. He was consistent as the high runs-batted-in man. In 1964, he led the league in RBIs with 118, while hitting 28 homers and batting .317. He was the American League's Most Valuable Player in 1964. After joining the club in 1955, he played 23 seasons with the Baltimore Orioles.

Robinson came to the Major Leagues shortly after his 18th birthday. He was up and down a few years before finally establishing himself as the regular Baltimore third baseman in the latter part of 1959. From 1960 through 1975, he never played less than 144 games in any season.

Even though he was slow afoot, the 6'1" 190-pounder managed to hit .300 in two separate seasons and finished with a lifetime average of .267. He had 100 or more RBIs in two separate seasons, and collected 2,848 hits during his brilliant career.

The soft-spoken southerner was a player-coach in his final season of 1977, after which he voluntarily retired.

In 1978, Brooks served as a broadcaster in Baltimore. Robinson must wait until January of 1983 before he is eligible for the Hall of Fame, but he certainly will make it. His glove, the one he used to defeat the Reds almost single-handed in the 1970 Series, already rests in Cooperstown.

BABE RUTH

Baseball's greatest slugger.

When Babe Ruth left baseball, the New York Yankees retired his famous Number 3 uniform forever. He had become a legend and no one could ever take the great Bambino's place.

Babe Ruth grew up as an orphan at Mount St. Michael school. He was taught how to handle a needle. He was supposed to become a tailor, but Brother Gilbert suspected otherwise. Apparently, young Ruth was a rather good hand at pitching a baseball.

In 1914, he was signed by the Baltimore Orioles. Soon, he was picked up by the Boston Americans for $2,500!

In a few seasons, it became clear that Babe Ruth was the best left-hander in the American League. He helped pitch the Red Sox to three world championships, chalking up a brilliant pitching record of 29⅔ consecutive scoreless World Series innings.

But his dazzling record as a pitcher was soon eclipsed by his spectacular slugging. In 1918, he tied for home run honors in the league with 11 home runs. In 1919, The Babe's great war club clouted out 29. Then Colonel Ruppert bought him for New York, and the Yanks converted him to an outfielder, so they could make full use of his hitting power.

Ruth knocked down record after record, each time setting up new ones only he could equal. During his 22 years in the major leagues, the Sultan of Swat hit 729 home runs, 15 of them in World Series play. Opposing pitchers were so afraid of Ruth that they walked him 2,056 times. In the 1923 season, Ruth received 170 base-on-balls.

In all, the Babe set up some 50 records. In the 1926 World Series, he socked three home runs in one game. In the 1928 World Series, he did it again, ringing up a total of 10 hits—the all-time high for a four-game Series. His batting average of .625 for that Series is still top mark for championship play.

Babe Ruth gave baseball dozens of new records; but more, Babe gave the game the warmth and color of his own personality. For the great Sultan of Swat—one might say, single-handed—launched big-time baseball into a new era of glory.

JOE DIMAGGIO

The Yankee clipper.

In 1948, the Bombers were battling the Bosox in a tough one. In the top of the tenth, the score stood 6-6. The Yanks had the bases full, with two out. There was a tense hush as Joe DiMaggio stepped into the batter's box. Earl Caldwell, Boston hurler, wound up and let fly. DiMag lashed out and sent a tremendous drive roaring into left field. It cleared the fence. In the press box, a writer expressed everybody's feelings when he said, "You don't hit two balls that hard in one time at bat."

He was wrong, because you do if your name is DiMaggio. The Yankee Clipper lashed into Caldwell's very next delivery. The center fielder got only a glimpse of the ball as it crash-landed high into the center field bleachers.

When the chips were down, DiMaggio was always a man to be reckoned with. As Joe explained it, "I figure the pitcher should be more worried than I am." And since Joe hit over 300 home runs in the big parks, he was probably right.

Joe's nonpareil mark is his matchless performance of 1941, when he hit safely in 56 consecutive games. From May 15th to July 16th, Joe gave every pitcher goose pimples. He hit safely in every game he played, and these were no baby taps, either. During his phenomenal streak, he registered 15 homers, 4 triples, and 16 doubles. His percentage on this grand march was a juicy .408. He had batted in 55 runs.

Though Joe led the league twice in batting and holds various and sundry records for hitting, DiMaggio may be said to have been the very best of recent outfielders. On defense, Joe was a manager's dream. Any ball arriving in center field found Joe planted under it, waiting to gather it into his glove. There weren't many gasps from the stands when DiMaggio made a catch! Joe made it look so easy.

Joe was your all-around player and the baseball magnates knew it. His salary of $100,000 in 1949 was probably the top salary ever earned by any player in the big time at that time. No doubt that the fans considered him the tops, too, for beginning with his first selection in 1936 for All-Star competition, Joe was chosen for this honor 12 times.

WILLIE MAYS

"I don't rate 'em, I just catch 'em."

In the 1954 World Series, first baseman Vic Wert of Cleveland hit a ball 460 feet in front of the center field clubhouse in the old Polo Grounds in New York. The Giants outfielder, Willie Mays, racing back to the deepest part of the park, caught the drive over his shoulder as he neared the clubhouse steps. Asked afterwards if he thought his catch was the greatest he had ever made, the youngster said, "I don't rate 'em, I just catch 'em."

It was that way throughout his amazing career. No ball that stayed in a ball park was uncatchable for the great outfielder. Mays hit 660 home runs—only Hank Aaron and Babe Ruth have hit more— and amassed a lifetime average of .302. He knocked in 1,903 runs and played regularly from the first day he joined the Giants in 1951 almost until he quit— after the 1973 season at age 42.

Perhaps it was not only his fielding, running, throwing, or hitting that made Mays so popular a player, and the most outstanding baseball player of his team. Few ever played the game with such boyish enthusiasm, with such excitement and drama.

He was named the National League rookie of the year in 1951, and he won the Most Valuable Player Award in 1954. In that year, he hit 51 homers. In 1965, at age 34, he hit 52.

Willie Howard Mays was born May 6, 1931 at Westfield, Alabama. His father had played some baseball and they were often together in neighborhood games. At 16, Willie was playing professional baseball in the old Negro Leagues. In 1951, at age 20, Willie joined the New York Giants as centerfielder under manager Leo Durocher.

In 1951, the Giants won the pennant on Bobby Thomson's playoff homer against the Dodgers with rookie Mays on deck. Willie helped the Giants win again in 1954 and in 1962.

Mays played for the New York Mets in the World Series of 1973. When he lost a fly ball in the sun against the Oakland A's, Mays knew it was time to quit. After the 1973 season, Mays joined the Mets as a batting coach.

CASEY STENGEL

The old professor.

On October 12, 1948, many people were shocked when Casey Stengel, after winning a pennant in Oakland, was named manager of the New York Yankees. Stengel had formerly managed the Brooklyn Dodgers and the Boston Braves without success.

Perhaps, his antics and his strange way of speaking—which came to be known as Stengelese—were as much a part of his makeup as his harsh voice, his bowed legs, his floppy ears, and his dedication to win.

Casey Stengel would go on to win 10 pennants in the next 12 years with the Yankees, and five World Series in a row—from 1949 through 1953—a feat never recorded before in baseball.

Born on July 30, 1890, Stengel had a career as a Major League player of some note. He was a fine defensive outfielder.

He started his pro career after leaving dental school in Kansas City. He joined the Brooklyn Dodgers in September 1912, and was traded to Pittsburgh, Philadelphia, the New York Giants, and the Boston Braves before becoming a minor league manager.

Stengel starred with the New York Giants as a part-time player winning two World Series games in 1923 against Babe Ruth's Yankees with an inside-the-park homer and a line-drive homer into the stands.

Casey returned to the Dodgers as a coach in 1932. He became the manager of the Brooklyn team in 1934. He was fired after the 1936 season, and took over the Boston Braves in 1938. He never finished higher than fifth with any of those teams.

Casey's lifetime batting average as a player was .284. He played from 1912 through 1925. He never lost interest in the game. At 85, he was still working as West Coast vice-president for the Mets.

He was installed in the Hall of Fame in 1966. Charles Dillon "Casey" Stengel, often known as The Old Professor, died in Glendale, California on September 29, 1975. The New York baseball writers established an award in his name called the "You Could Look It Up Award." Casey was always saying of baseball records, "You could look it up." Baseball fans are well advised to look up his.

Tris Speaker

Honus Wagner

Frank Baker

THE ALL-STAR TEAM
OF THE EARLY PERIOD
(1900-1920)

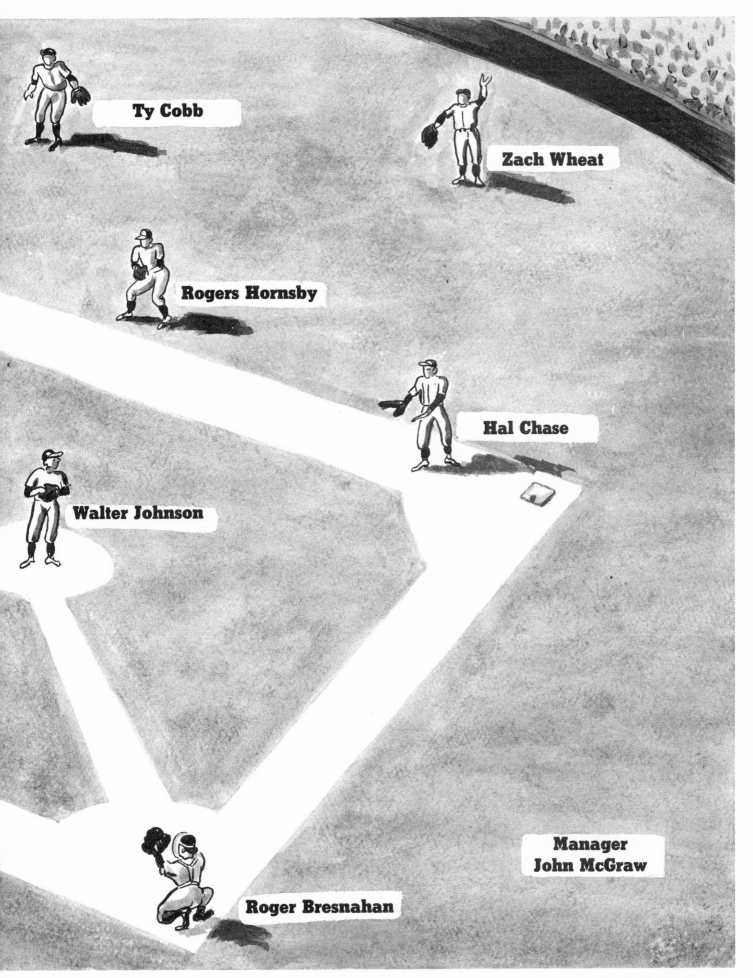

Ty Cobb

Zach Wheat

Rogers Hornsby

Hal Chase

Walter Johnson

Roger Bresnahan

Manager
John McGraw

NOTES ON THE SELECTIONS OF THE ALL-STAR TEAM OF THE EARLY PERIOD (1900-1920)

According to the pundits, Walter Johnson was the best of the old pitchers, but Christy Mathewson, the Giant immortal, finished a strong second.

Ray Schalk, who caught from 1912 through 1929, was runner-up to Roger Bresnahan.

Hal Chase, who hit .291 from 1905 through 1919 and was considered the best fielder in the game at his position, finished second to Frank Chance at first base.

Eddie Colins, a Hall of Famer, was ranked behind Rogers Hornsby at second base.

At shortstop, Rabbit Maranville finished second to Honus Wagner.

Bill McKechnie, later to gain fame as manager, was the runner-up at third base to "Home Run" Baker.

Harry Heilmann of the Detroit Tigers just missed out in the outfield, finishing only two votes behind Zach Wheat in one of the closest decisions. The easy winners, Cobb and Speaker, led all the way. Joe Jackson, Sam Crawford, Elmer Flick, and Edd Roush also came in as runners-up.

Wilbert Robinson, who won pennants in Brooklyn in 1916 and 1920, finished second behind John McGraw as the best manager in the era.

ROGER BRESNAHAN

JOHN MCGRAW

THE RUNNERS-UP

Christy Mathewson, *Pitcher*

Ray Schalk, *Catcher*

Hal Chase, *First Baseman*

Eddie Collins, *Second Baseman*

Rabbit Maranville, *Shortstop*

Bill McKechnie, *Third Baseman*

Harry Heilmann, *Outfielder*

Joe Jackson, *Outfielder*

Sam Crawford, *Outfielder*

Elmer Flick, *Outfielder*

Edd Roush, *Outfielder*

Wilbert Robinson, *Manager*

Ted Williams

Joe Cronin

Pie Traynor

THE ALL-STAR TEAM
OF THE MIDDLE PERIOD
(1920-1960)

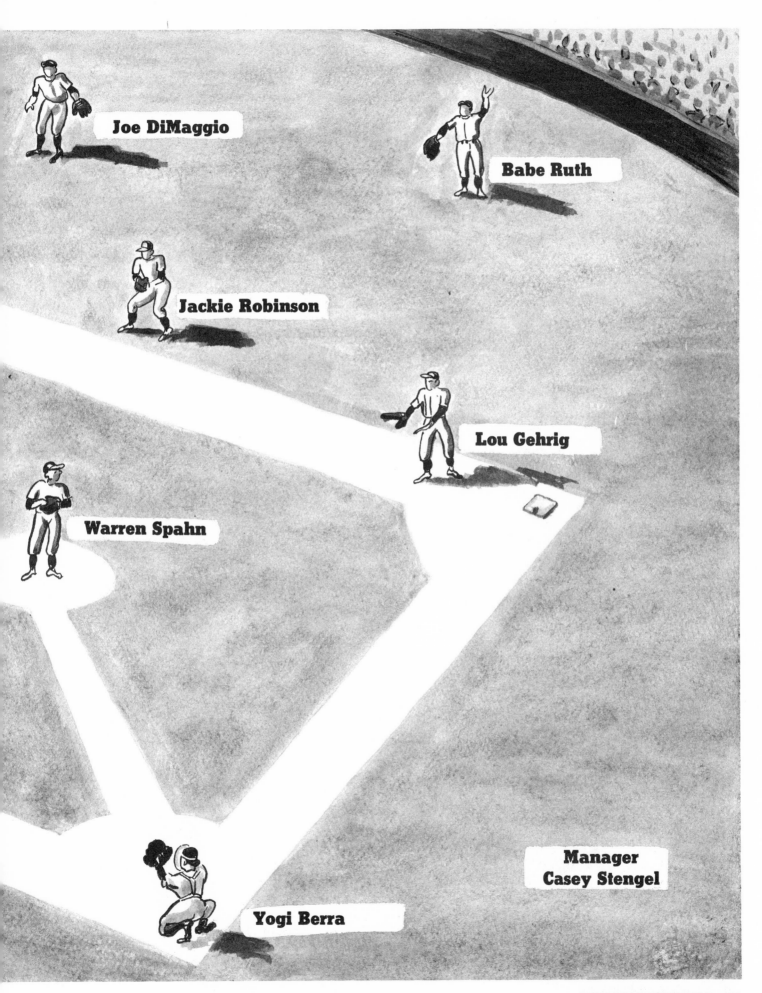

NOTES ON THE SELECTIONS OF
THE ALL-STAR TEAM OF
THE MIDDLE PERIOD (1920-1960)

The longest period covered—1920 through 1960—caused the most disagreement. Babe Ruth changed the game with his 54 homers in 1920. Baseball also changed with its expansion in 1961.

Behind Warren Spahn, the runner-up pitcher was Bob Feller, the great righthander of the Cleveland Indians.

Mickey Cochrane ran close behind Yogi Berra for the star catcher.

Stan Musial, a .331 lifetime hitter, was runner-up to Lou Gehrig, who won in a landslide for first base.

Frankie Frisch, the Fordam Flash, one of the great switch-hitters of all time, was runner-up to Jackie Robinson for second base.

Luis Aparicio was a strong contender for shortstop honors, but lost out to Joe Cronin.

Eddie Mathews finished behind Pie Traynor for third base.

DiMaggio, Ruth, and Williams dominated the voting for the fielding positions. Mickey Mantle, Frank Robinson, and Duke Snider put on a strong show.

Casey Stengel edged Joe McCarthy as best manager during this period.

TED WILLIAMS

MICKEY MANTLE

THE RUNNERS-UP

Bob Feller, *Pitcher*   **Eddie Mathews,** *Third Baseman*

Mickey Cochrane, *Catcher*   **Mickey Mantle,** *Outfielder*

Stan Musial, *First Baseman*   **Frank Robinson,** *Outfielder*

Frank Frisch, *Second Baseman*   **Duke Snider,** *Outfielder*

Luis Aparicio, *Shortstop*   **Harry Heilmann,** *Outfielder*

Joe McCarthy, *Manager*

Willie Mays

Maury Wills

Brooks Robinson

THE ALL-STAR TEAM
OF THE MODERN PERIOD
1961-1978

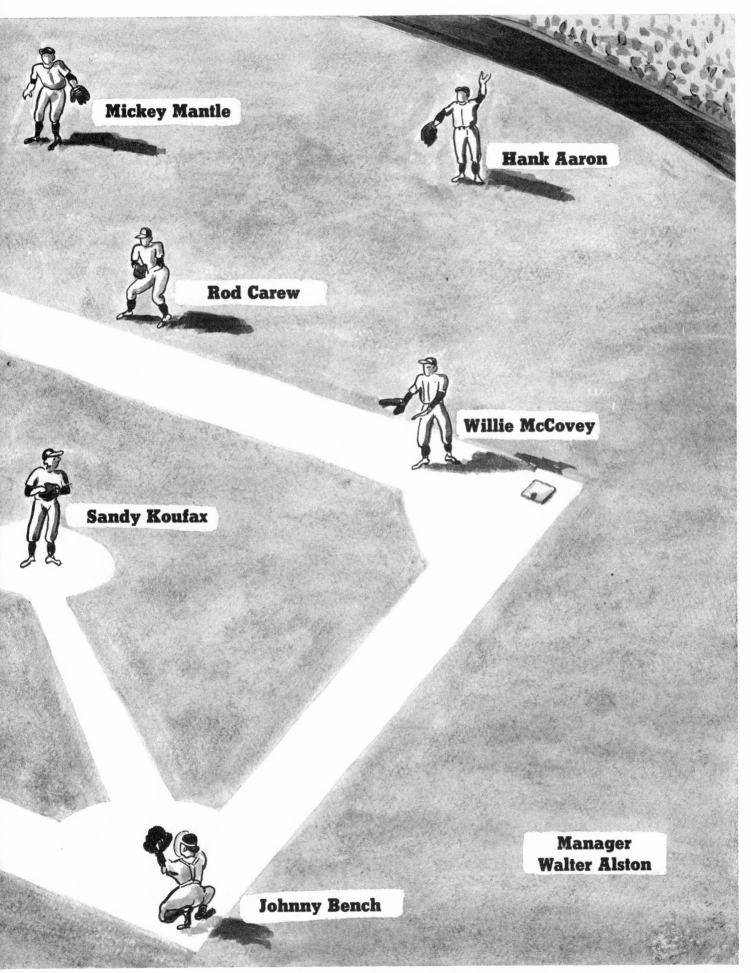

Mickey Mantle

Hank Aaron

Rod Carew

Willie McCovey

Sandy Koufax

Manager
Walter Alston

Johnny Bench

NOTES ON THE SELECTIONS OF THE ALL-STAR TEAM OF THE MODERN PERIOD (1961-1978)

The races among the modern players were surprisingly one-sided. Sandy Koufax with 126 votes, was an easy winner over Jim Palmer, who gathered 13 votes for pitcher.

Yankee catcher Thurman Munson with 42 votes, was a long way behind Johnny Bench, who had 88 votes. Steve Garvey, with 56 votes, lost to Giants first baseman Willie McCovey who received 71 votes.

For second base, Rod Carew was an easy winner. Joe Morgan was his nearest challenger. Maury Wills at shortstop was a shoo-in with Dave Concepcion finishing second. Surprisingly, there were 17 write-in votes for Larry Bowa of the Phillies, the most write-ins for any player in this entire balloting.

Brooks Robinson edged Pete Rose for third baseman, but Rose might have more opportunities in a future election.

Roberto Clemente, the late outfielder of the Pirates, finished fourth in outfield with 55 votes. Frank Robinson, Carl Yastrzemski, and Tony Oliva followed. Al Kaline received 13 write-ins.

For manager, Walter Alston of the Dodgers was a big winner. Earl Weaver of the Orioles finished second.

HANK AARON

JOE MORGAN

THE RUNNERS-UP

Jim Palmer, *Pitcher*   Roberto Clemente, *Outfielder*

Thurman Munson, *Catcher*   Frank Robinson, *Outfielder*

Steve Garvey, *First Baseman*   Carl Yastrzemski, *Outfielder*

Joe Morgan, *Second Baseman*   Tony Oliva, *Outfielder*

Dave Concepcion, *Shortstop*   Al Kaline, *Outfielder*

Pete Rose, *Third Baseman*   Earl Weaver, *Manager*

THE HALL OF RECORDS

Mike Marshall relief-pitched in 106 games.

During the 1974 season, the Los Angeles Dodgers played in only 56 games without their fine relief pitcher, Mike Marshall, making an appearance.

Marshall, a physical fitness professor from the University of Michigan, was strong enough to appear in 106 games, a record for relief pitchers. He did not start a single game, but was 15-12 with 208 innings pitched.

Yastrzemski won a batting crown with only a .301 average.

Carl Yastrzemski has batted .301 on two separate occasions in his long and distinguished career. In 1968, he batted .301 for the Boston Red Sox and won the batting title, the lowest figure for a batting leader in Major League history.

(In 1974, he came back with his second .301 mark. But this time he was 63 points behind Rod Carew, the batting leader.)

Devore stole four bases in one inning.

When it comes to freewheeling on the basepaths, no one has ever matched the record of Josh Devore, old-time Giant outfielder.

On June 20, 1912, in the ninth inning of a game against the Braves, Josh came up to bat. He reached first safely and then stole second. Then he went ahead and stole third.

That's pretty enough. But the New Yorkers had a terrific inning, and batted all through the batting order. When Josh got up again, he repeated his entire performance.

That made a total of four stolen bases in one inning!

Smith hit seven extra-base hits in a row.

On September 4 and 5, 1921, Cleveland right fielder Elmer Smith displayed something extra in the extra-base line. In seven consecutive times at bat, Smith drove out seven extra-baggers—four home runs and three doubles.

Elmer got himself a baseball record.

Bottomley drove in 12 runs in one game.

On September 16, 1924, first baseman Jim Bottomley, of the St. Louis Cardinals, set a major league mark by driving in a dozen tallies in a single game.

Here's that Jim-dandy record:

1st inning:	Jim singled;	drove in 2 runs.
2nd inning:	Jim doubled;	drove in 1 run.
4rd inning:	Jim homered;	drove in 4 runs.
6th inning:	Jim homered;	drove in 2 runs.
7th inning:	Jim singled;	drove in 2 runs.
9th inning:	Jim singled;	drove in 1 run.

Bottomley's feat that afternoon also put him in a tie for the major league record of six hits by a batter in a nine-inning game.

Burnett made nine hits in one game.

In Cleveland on July 10, 1932, the Indians and the Athletics staged a farce in 18 acts which they deceptively labeled a ball game.

The hero of this melange was Cleveland shortstop Johnny Burnett, who labored manfully in the batter's box to snag nine hits—the all-time major league record for a single game.

Alas! Burnett's yeoman service availed naught. Cleveland lost by a score at once close and grotesque. At the end of 18 innings, the final count stood Philadelphia 18, Cleveland 17.

In the prodigious proceedings, some statistics are worthy of passing interest. The Indians scored 33 safe hits; the Athletics a mere 25. This totaled 58 safeties in a single game! The winning pitcher was reliever Ed Rommel, who allowed—hold on to your hat—29 hits!

Ott scored six runs in one game.

On August 4, 1934, Mel Ott, great outfield star of the New York Giants, became the first ballplayer of modern times to score six runs in a nine-inning game. To prove it wasn't an accident, Mel repeated the performance 10 years later.

Ott's sextette has since been equaled; but only Mel has two such scoring marathons to his credit.

The Cubs and the Phillies
made 51 hits in one game.

It happened on August 25, 1922. The tallies came in so thick and fast no one knew who succumbed more quickly, the pitchers or the score-keepers.

In the wild-scoring melee, the Cubs came out on the long end of a 26-23 count.

It will surprise practically no one to learn that another all-time record was set during the same nine innings. The Phillies slapped out 26 safeties and the Cubs 25, a total of 51 raps in one slap-happy game.

Foxx got six base-on-balls in one game.

On June 16, 1938, Jimmy Foxx stood in the batter's box six times, yet the official records do not credit him with a single time at bat! For on that day, opposing pitchers presented the Red Sox slugger with six bases on balls, a major league record.

Jimmy led both leagues in batting that year, and knocked in 175 runs. It's easy to see why pitchers were plenty afraid of the big, bad Foxx!

Gehrig hit four home runs in four consecutive at bats.

On June 3, 1932, Lou Gehrig, the Pride of the Yankees, hit four home runs in four consecutive times at bat for the Yankees. A feat worthy of front-page position in most papers in America.

But Lou chose to execute his incredible hitting feat on the very day that John McGraw, the famous manager of the Giants, decided to quit. The newspapers were filled with long biographies of McGraw, long stories about his winning teams, and long lists of his players. And the quiet man of the Yankees, Lou Gehrig, received skimpy news space for his slugging that day.

Grover Cleveland Alexander pitched 16 shutouts in one season.

"Old Pete" marched through the National League hitters in 1916 like Sherman through Atlanta. He was burning 'em up.

Alexander won 33 games for the Philadelphia Phillies that year and turned in 16 shutouts.

Marquard won 19 games in a row.

Rube Marquard was once called "The $10,000 lemon" because he was purchased from the minor leagues for that huge price in 1908, and proceeded to win no games at all in 1908, only five games in 1909, and only four games in 1920, while pitching for New York. In 1911, he found his pitching style, and won 24 games, losing only seven.

In 1912, he set a record by winning 19 games in a row at the start of the season, a mark that still stands. In 1978, Ron Guidry of the New York Yankees came close, when he started the season by winning his first 14 games in a row.

After Marquard won his 19 games, he finished the season with a mark of 26-11 as he and his pal, Christy Mathewson, pitched the Giants to the National League pennant.

Gehrig played in 2,130 consecutive games.

Stan Musial owns the National League mark. Musial played in 895 games from opening day 1952 until June 12, 1957. A shoulder injury finally moved "The Man" to the bench.

The Major League record for consecutive games played is 2,130 by Lou Gehrig.

Wynn pitched for 23 seasons.

Early Wynn won 300 games in his distinguished career in the American League. He played with some poor ball clubs in Washington and in Chicago, and with some medicore clubs in Cleveland. Wherever Early played, he almost always wound up winning 20 games a season.

The most important thing about this pitcher was that he was still winning at age 43 for the Cleveland Indians.

Wynn put in 23 seasons in the American League, a record that's not likely to be matched.

The Giants beat the Phillies in 51 minutes.

Almost as fast as you can read this, the Giants beat the Phillies 6-1 in a nine-inning game that lasted only 51 minutes. Whew!

Frederick hit six pinch-hit home runs in one season.

Johnny Frederick of the Brooklyn Dodgers was one of those guys you could wake up in January and he'd hit a home run. A part-time outfielder for the Brooklyn Dodgers, Frederick hit six pinch-hit home runs for Brooklyn in the 1932 season.

Eddie Collins stole six bases in one game.

On September 11, 1912, Eddie Collins of the Philadelphia A's stole six bases against the Detroit Tigers in one game.

And in a game against the St. Louis Browns, he did it again—six bases in one game!

Gibson's earned run average in 1968 was 1.12.

Bob Gibson had a frightening pitching motion—frightening for the hitter—as he fell off the mound and fired his fastball at the hitters.

He was the toughest of all in 1968. In that season, he won 22 games, lost nine, and turned in an earned run average of 1.12, the best in baseball history.

In more than 300 innings, he recorded 13 shutouts and 268 strikeouts.

Four Yankee pitchers hit home runs with the bases full.

Four pitchers in New York Yankee history were able to smash grand slam home runs during their careers. Red Ruffing was the first to do it in 1933; Spud Chandler did it in 1940; Don Larsen accomplished the feat in 1955; and Mel Stottlemyre came through in 1965.

Carl Hubbell won 24 games in a row in two seasons.

Carl Hubbell, the screwballing lefthander of the Giants, recorded the most consecutive wins of any pitcher in the history of the game. From July 17, 1936 through May 27, 1937, Hubbell won 24 games for the Giants. No one has ever come close to that mark.

Johnny Allen and Dave McNally share the American League record with 17 straight wins, Allen turning in that figure with the Indians in 1936 and 1937, and McNally winning that many for the Baltimore Orioles in 1968 and 1969.

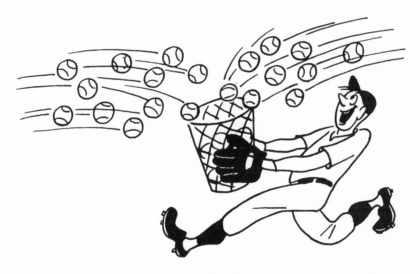

Eddie Joost fielded 19 balls on one afternoon.

On May 7, 1941, shortstop Eddie Joost of the Cincinnati Reds must have felt some stinging in his hands. He manages to field 19 balls cleanly that day with nine putouts and ten assists.

He couldn't quite make it on chance number 20. He threw away one ground ball for an error—to keep from having a perfect day.

Seaver strikes out 19 in one game.

On April 22, 1970, you could feel the breeze from Flushing Meadow all over New York and throughout the cities in the National League.

A year after the Mets had won a miracle pennant in 1969—led by two young pitchers—Tom Seaver and Jerry Koosman—the righhanded half of the dynamic duo, Seaver, was pitching against the San Diego Padres.

"I felt good warming up," remembers Seaver. "I knew I would have a good fastball that day. But I couldn't imagine it would be that good."

Who could imagine it? Seaver struck out every batter in the San Diego lineup. He averaged more than two strikeouts an inning, as he recorded 19 strikeouts.

The incredible aspect of the entire performance was that he struck out the last 10 San Diego batters in a row. When he was supposed to be weakening, he was getting stronger.

Fisk walloped out nine triples in 1972.

The husky catcher of the Boston Red Sox, Carlton Fisk, hit nine triples in 1972, a record for catchers that is likely to remain for a long time.

Ott walked five times in one game.

When he came to the New York Giants as a 16-year-old schoolboy out of high school, Mel Ott—called Master Melvin by the press—was put under the wing of manager John McGraw, who kept Master Melvin snug on the bench next to him.

When McGraw finally let him loose, Mel proved to be one of the great sluggers of all time. He hit 511 homers during a great career. The lad also knew a ball from a strike, and walked 1,708 times.

In fact, in four different games, Mel Ott walked as many as five times.

Musial made 3,630 hits during his career.

In 1939, Stan Musial was pitching in the minor leagues. He came up with a sore arm, and many people figured he was finished as a ball player.

His manager, Dickie Kerr, had seen him bat, and suggested Musial try staying in the game with his bat.

Two years later, Stan won in the big leagues. In 1943, he won his first batting title with a .357 mark. He was to win six more before he quit in 1963.

Before he was through, Musial would record 3,630 hits, a National League record.

Adams pitched 21 innings on one afternoon and never walked a man.

One July 17, 1914, Charles B. Adams of the Pittsburgh Pirates, pitched 21 innings and did not walk a single man.

Denton True "Cy" Young had set the American League mark, when he pitched 20 innings for the Red Sox on July 4, 1905, and didn't issue a single pass.

Sisler registered 257 hits in a single season.

George Sisler batted .407 in 1920 when playing for the St. Louis Browns. No man has ever recorded more hits in one season.

Babe Ruth got 170 walks in one season.

Don't pitch to the Babe. That was the word around the American League from 1920 on, as Babe Ruth began hitting home runs in record numbers. The pitchers, unable to control the Babe's bat, began to do the only thing that was guaranteed to stop him. They started walking him.

In 1923, it got ridiculous as the Babe set a record with 170 walks.

Ruth also managed to hit 41 homers that year when they were walking him, and struck out 93 times.

In 1906, the Yanks
won five doubleheaders in a row.

One of the toughest feats in baseball is to win a doubleheader. This is because players become tired after one game, relief pitchers wear out, and the fans become noisy. None of this bothered the New York Yankees in 1906.

In a record of excellence that probably can never be touched, the New Yorkers marched through five straight doubleheaders with nary a loss.

They beat the Washington Senators on August 30, August 31, and September 1 for six games straight. They rested on September 2. On September 3, they beat the Philadelphia Athletics in a twin bill, and proceeded to make a clean sweep that week by wiping out the Boston Red Sox in both games of a doubleheader.

Five days, ten games, ten wins, and tired bones.

Valo, a pinch hitter,
was walked 18 times in one season.

Pinch hitters are sent to the plate with the tying or winning runs on base. They are asked to drive the runner home.

But sometimes there is nothing a batter can do about it. In 1960, Elmer Valo was walked 18 times in his pinch-hitting appearances for the Yankees and the Washington Senators.

Reiser stole home
seven times in a single season.

In 1946, Pete Reiser of the Brooklyn Dodgers stole home seven times in a single season. The mark was equalled by Rod Carew of the Minnesota Twins in 1969.

Power stole home twice in a single game.

Vic Power was a delightful, baldheaded, hard-hitting, slick-fielding first baseman. He loved to grab a foul ball out of the stands with one flick of his wrist. He also loved to run.

On August 14, 1958, he stole home twice in a single game, a feat that hadn't been pulled off for 47 years.

Frank Robinson won the
Most Valuable Player award in two leagues.

The most prestigious award in baseball is the *Most Valuable Player* trophy, awarded annually by the Baseball Writers Association of America.

Only one man in the history of the award, dating back to 1931, when Lefty Grove won the trophy in the American League, and Frankie Frisch won the trophy in the National League, has ever been able to switch leagues and perform just as well.

Frank Robinson led the Cincinnati Reds to the pennant in 1961. Five years later, he was traded to the Baltimore Orioles. And he led *them* to a pennant.

In both seasons—1961 as a Red, and 1966 as an Oriole—Robinson was his league's Most Valuable Player. Unbelievable!

The Yanks left 20 men
on base in a single game.

On September 21, 1956, the Yankees were playing against their old rivals, the Boston Red Sox. The Yankees were having a big hitting day. They smacked out 18 hits, and scored 13 runs, and won 13-7.

What was fantastic that day was the men that didn't score, not the ones who did.

With all that hitting, the Yankees managed to leave 20 men on base for a record.

Brock stole 118 bases in 1974.

Lou Brock holds the record for most stolen bases in a season with his 118 in 1974. He also holds the record for most failures in stealing bases, when in that same season, he was thrown out 33 times.

On the other hand, Max Carey stole 51 bases one season and was thrown out only twice. From 1913 through 1925, for 10 seasons, Carey led his league in larceny.

Vander Meer pitched two consecutive no-hitters.

When you are the only player to record a record in the big leagues, that is something very special. There are few records and few feats more special than the performance of high-kicking Johnny Vander Meer of the Cincinnati Reds on June 11 and June 15, 1938.

On the first day, Vander Meer, pitching in Boston, beat the Braves 3-0 without allowing a hit. He gave up three walks, and two of the batters were retired on double plays. The 22-year-old lefthander faced only 28 men.

That feat alone would have put him in very select baseball company. But as Al Jolson used to say, "You ain't heard nuthin' yet."

On June 15, the Brooklyn Dodgers inaugurated night baseball in Ebbets Field. On that evening, under a perfectly clear sky, the lights were turned on. So was Vander Meer. He was a little wilder against the Dodgers, and allowed eight walks, but nary a batter could get a bingle. The baseball world gasped. A second no-hitter. Two *consecutive* no-hitters! A feat never recorded before or since.

The closest try was turned in by Ewell Blackwell, also of Cincinnati, on June 18 and June 22, 1947. He pitched a no-hitter against those same Braves, and almost duplicated against those same Dodgers. Blackwell went 8⅓ innings before Eddie Stanky and Jackie Robinson slapped singles through the middle. Blackwell missed his second straight no-hitter and Vander Meer stood alone.

Johnny (Double No-Hit) probably will always stand alone.

THE HALL OF WONDERS

Pete Gray played baseball with only one hand.

During World War II, most healthy ball players were off in the Army. The St. Louis Browns needed anybody they could get. In 1945, they brought up a one-armed outfielder by the name of Pete Gray!

Gray used to bat with that one hand, and catch with that one hand, and throw with it, too. He would catch a fly ball in his left hand, throw the ball into the air, stick the glove under his right stump, catch the ball bare-handed, and throw it back to the infield.

Gray managed to hit .218 in 77 games.

Richardson drove in 12 runs during the 1960 World Series.

Bobby Richardson was a smallish second baseman for the Yankees, famed for his good glove.

In 1960, he showed he was more than just a fielder, as he drove in 12 runs in the World Series against the Pittsburgh Pirates. It was some performance. It was made even more notable by the fact that Richardson had batted in only 26 runs in a season of 150 games.

The Chicago Cubs won a pennant with a .763 average.

In 1906, the Chicago Cubs whisked through a 154-game season with only 38 losses. They won 116 games, recorded a percentage of .763, and finished 20 games ahead of the second place Giants.

But these hotshots somehow managed to lose four games out of six in the World Series to their south side rivals in Chicago, the White Sox.

McGinnity pitched and won three doubleheaders in one month.

The pitcher who has to be coddled with three or four days rest after every mound assignment just walks off to union headquarters when you mention the name of "Iron Man" McGinnity.

For that famous old pitcher was well-nigh indestructible, and would have laughed down his pitching sleeve at today's crop of tissue-paper athletes. McGinnity could pitch day after day without any apparent strain. In August of 1903, Joe McGinnity, wearing a Giant uniform, pitched three full doubleheaders. He won all six games!

In one of these encounters, McGinnity allowed only one run. In two others, he held the opposition to two runs. In another, he yielded three tallies. And one afternoon, carrying a twin-pitching burden, Joe helped win a close one by stealing home with a vital run.

When Joe McGinnity was 54 years old, The Iron Man was still taking a regular turn for the Dubuque team in the Missouri Valley League.

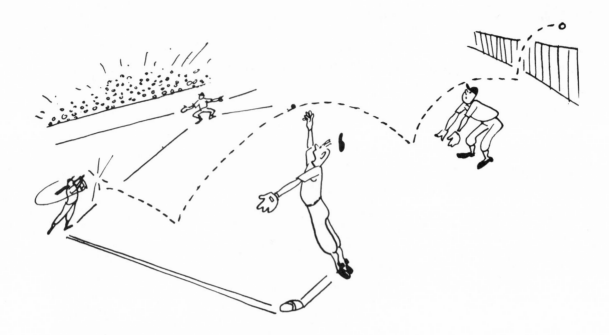

Grounder defies gravity.

In 1916, George Cutshaw, Dodger second baseman, broke up a ball-game with a ground ball that miraculously climbed over the fence for a home run!

The Dodgers were playing the Phillies at Ebbets Field in a hard-fought, extra-inning game. With the score tied in the last half of the eleventh, Cutshaw slammed a hot grass-clipping drive into right field—a hard-hit ball worth two bases in any league.

But Cutshaw's grounder was marked for high destiny. As the Phila-delphia right fielder charged in to field the ball off the fence, the sphe-roid struck the embankment, and instead of caroming off the fence, continued to roll upward—urged on by some sort of English. The ball actually climbed the fence!

For a moment, the ball teetered at the top as if to taunt the Phillie fielder, and then it hopped over.

The Dodgers won the game. Cutshaw's smash had gone down in baseball history as the only ground ball that ever rolled outside a major league ballpark. And in those days, a ball that cleared the fence on however many bounces was a homer, not a ground-rule double.

The things that can happen in Brooklyn!

Rookie hits two homers in his first two at bats.

On September 14, 1951, Bob Nieman stepped to the plate for his first time in the big leagues. As usual, the St. Louis Browns were mired in the second division, and had brought up their farm phenoms for a look-see.

Nieman may have been terrified on his first trip to the plate, but he got a pitch in his power zone and belted it over the wall. Evidently, the rookie outfielder enjoyed the cheers of the fans, for the next time up, he banged out another homer. No rookie has ever matched this feat.

No-hitter revenge.

On the night of September 17, 1968, Gaylord Perry hurled a no-hitter against the St. Louis Cardinals at Candlestick Park. The Cardinals wasted no time exacting their revenge, as Ray Washburn set down the Giants without a hit on the following afternoon.

Never in the history of baseball had teams traded no-hitters on consecutive days. But like the four-minute mile, once the swap was accomplished, it suddenly became easy.

Next year, on April 30, Jim Maloney of Cincinnati held the Astros without a hit. On May 1—the very next day—Houston's Don Wilson returned the favor.

Lucky hit.

In 1936, the Brooklynites were losing game after game in a disastrous slump. One afternoon during pregame practice, Frenchy Bordagaray accidentally beaned manager Casey Stengel with a thrown ball. In order not to further upset the team's already frazzled nerves, Casey heroically kept his temper.

That day, while a lump grew in Brooklyn, the Dodgers won.

After the game, Frenchy buttonholed Stengel in the clubhouse. "Casey," he said, "I think we got the answer. Just for luck, let me hit you on the head before every game. Then maybe we'll keep on winning."

Paige pitched when he was 59.

In 1965, Satchel Paige, who was originally hired as a coach, left his bullpen rocking chair, and made a pitching appearance for the Kansas City A's. He was just short of his 60th birthday, give or take a couple of years for fibs.

Old Satchel never quite gave his real age because he lived by the creed, "Never look back because something might be gaining on you."

Before Satch, the record had been held by Nick Altrock, a coach with the Washington Senators. He had gotten into a game on October 1, 1933, at age 57.

How his bones creaked after that afternoon.

Smallest crowd to witness a major league ball game.

On September 27, 1881, the Chicago White Stockings were in Troy, New York—then a National League franchise—to play the final game of the season. The Sox had long since clinched the pennant, Troy was locked in fifth place, and the rain was coming down in diluvial fashion. Yet for some mysterious reason, these three incentives not to play the game failed to deter the participants, and Chicago and Troy sloshed on to a conclusion.

What is even more mysterious is that anyone paid good money to see this game. But twelve hardy idiots did, and thus put themselves into the record books as the smallest paid crowd ever to witness any major league ball game.

Reynolds pitched two no-hitters in one season.

On July 12, 1951, Allie Reynolds of the Yankees pitched a no-hitter against the Cleveland Indians.

On September 28, he had a no-hitter going against the Boston Red Sox. There were two out in the ninth, and the powerful Ted Williams came to bat.

No pitcher had ever pitched two no-hitters in the American League in one season, although Johnny Vander Meer of Cincinnati had done it in the National League.

Reynolds got the great Williams to pop up to the catcher.

Dynamic duo wins 17 out of 18 starts.

The New York Mets made a fantastic comeback in 1969 to win the pennant in a long chase with Leo Durocher's Cubs. Every member of the Mets contributed mightily to that victory. But Tom Seaver and Jerry Koosman, two young pitchers, contributed the most.

From mid-August until the end of the season, starting 18 times, these two pitchers won 17 of 18 decisions.

A ground ball was lost in the sun.

Billy Loes was a fine pitcher for the Brooklyn Dodgers back in the early 1950s. He started a game in the 1952 World Series, and was moving along smoothly against the Yankees until a strange thing happened.

With a man on first and a man on third, Yogi Berra hit a hard, high bouncer back to the mound. The ball came right at Loes, who ducked away as the ball bounced over his head and into center field for a hit.

"What happened on that play?" a reporter asked Loes.

"I lost the ball in the sun," he said.

The reporters laughed and Loes was marked as a strange one after that. Lose a ground ball in the sun?

Yep, it could happen. Later a reporter went onto the field and asked the groundskeepers about the angle of the sun around the time Loes was pitching.

"Right up there behind the stands," said one.

Loes was right. A ground ball could be lost in the sun if he looked up for it. A wonder of wonders.

Three players have played in four decades.

Not many ball players make it through the big leagues for ten years. A very few make it for 15, and a select small group last 20.

It is a great achievement to play in four decades. In modern baseball, only three players—Ted Williams, Early Wynn, and Mickey Vernon—were able to play in big league games in four decades: the 1930s, the 1940s, the 1950s, and the 1960s.

Ron Fairly, who began his career with the Los Angeles Dodgers in 1958, will join that select group in 1980 after playing in the 50s, the 60s, the 70s and the 80s.

The Dodgers played 33 innings in the 1966 World Series without scoring a run.

The Los Angeles Dodgers of 1966 were a fine team with brilliant pitching led by Sandy Koufax and Don Drysdale.

They met the Baltimore Orioles that year and were beaten 5-2 in the opening game of the Series. The Dodgers scored one run in the second inning and one run in the third inning.

After that, it was Katy bar the door.

The Dodgers were shut out 6-0 in the second game, 1-0 in the third game, and 1-0 in the fourth game.

They had gone 33 straight innings without a Dodger batter touching his little toe on home plate. Talk about hitless and scoreless wonders—wow!

Managers rather switch than fight.

It was mid-season, 1960, and neither the Detroit Tigers nor the Cleveland Indians were going anywhere. Following traditional front-office policy, each club figured it was time to fire the manager. While Detroit cut loose Jimmie Dykes, Cleveland dismissed Joe Gordon. Dykes was immediately signed to pilot the Indians, and Gordon took over the Tiger helm.

The bizarre managerial shift made good copy on the sports pages, but it did little to help either ball club. Both Cleveland and Detroit finished under .500.

The Yanks won 10 pennants in 12 seasons.

Casey Stengel was considered a clown when he joined the Yankees as manager of the club in 1949, and a genius when he left in 1960.

What happened in between?

What happened was this: The Yankees won 10 pennants in 12 years under Stengel. Five of these pennants were consecutive—from 1949 through 1953.

In 1954, the Yanks won more games, 103, than they had ever won before under Stengel, but managed to finish only second. The Cleveland Indians won 111 that year.

The Dodgers had a "30-30-30-30" club.

In newspaper offices, the numbers 30 are used to indicate the end of a story.

For the Los Angeles Dodgers of 1977, the numbers 30 meant only home runs.

Steve Garvey had 33, Reggie Smith had 32, Dusty Baker had 30, and Ron Cey had 30. No Major League team—not even the Yankees of Ruth, Gehrig, and Company—ever had four players on the team in the same season, each of whom had hit 30 homers.

Phillippe won three games in a World Series, and wound up on the losing side.

The World Series, first played in 1903, was notable for a pitching performance by Charles Louis Phillippe of the Pittsburgh Pirates. He started five games, won three of the first four, and still wound up on the losing side as Boston won the Series.

The best pitcher for the Boston Red Sox was Cy Young, the man many people consider the best pitcher in baseball's earliest days, and the winningest pitcher of all time.

Spahn started a winning career at 25.

Warren Spahn recorded a lifetime mark of 363 wins against 245 losses in his career with the Braves, the Mets, and the San Francisco Giants.

In 1942, at age 21, he joined the Boston Braves under manager Casey Stengel. He finished his career under Stengel, with the Mets.

"I played for Casey before and after he was a genius," declared Spahn.

In 1942, Stengel wasn't enough of a genius to recognize the ability in the lefthander. He sent him to the minor leagues without giving him much of a chance.

Spahn entered military service for the years 1943, 1944, and 1945, and wound up with a distinguished war record in Europe.

He returned to the Braves in 1946, won eight games and lost five. He then proceeded to put together thirteen 20-game-winning seasons, retiring in 1966 at the age of 45.

Ed Kranepool played 50 innings in 27 hours.

Baseball's endurance record belongs to Ed Kranepool. He compiled the mark in two cities, in four games, over two leagues at the age of 19.

It all started on May 30, 1964, when Kranepool played in a doubleheader for the Buffalo farm team of the New York Mets. After he had finished 18 innings for Buffalo, he was told he was needed in New York with the Mets. Being recalled to the majors means hurrying to the bus terminal or airport as fast as you can pack a suitcase.

Kranepool was driven from the Buffalo ball park at 11:30 that night for a midnight flight to Newark. He arrived at 6 o'clock in the morning.

"I had a baloney sandwich out of a machine and then caught a cab for Shea Stadium. I got there somewhere after 7:30 in the morning, and went to sleep on the training table for the 1 o'clock doubleheader."

Casey Stengel started the young man at first base in the first game against the Giants. The Mets lost that one, of course, and Kranepool started again in the second game.

This one lasted 23 innings, and 7 hours and 23 minutes, with the Mets losing, 8-6. They had lost the first game 5-3. The doubleheader took 9 hours and 52 minutes.

Kranepool had played 50 innings, been on the field for more than 14 hours, and had very little sleep since he first put on his uniform in Buffalo.

"I went home," he said, "and the only thing I found to eat in the refrigerator was—a baloney sandwich."

Nobody could blank those Yankees.

The Yankees have so many records, it would take a computer to sort them all out. But a couple of them are likely to last forever.

From 1949 through 1953, under Casey Stengel, the Yankees won five pennants and five World Series in a row. In recent years only Oakland has come close to that record with three in a row, from 1972-1974.

Maybe the best Yankee team ever was the 1936 Yankees. But for scoring runs, how about the Yankees of 1931, 1932, and 1933. That team went from August 2, 1931 through August 3, 1933—two years and a day—without ever being shut out.

Lefty Grove, a Hall of Fame lefthander, won the honors of breaking the Yankees streak in 1933 with a 4-0 win.

Sutton lost 13 in a row to the Cubs.

The excellent righthander of Los Angeles Dodgers, Don Sutton, broke in with the Dodgers by pitching against the Chicago Cubs. He lost. He then proceeded to lose a total of 13 straight times to the Cubs before he finally recorded a win against them. It is a record that ran from April 23, 1966 to July 24, 1969.

Obviously, Sutton just doesn't like baby bears.

There are 24 Yankees enshrined in the Hall of Fame.

The New York Yankees have won more pennants than any other club.

Naturally, they lead the league in Hall of Fame players. Of the 135 players enshrined in the Cooperstown Hall of Fame, no less than 24 wore Yankee uniforms.

Sandy, you're a dandy!

The Brooklyn Dodgers must have had some doubts after signing Sandy Koufax in 1955. For five seasons, they were getting very little out of him.

Finally, in 1959, Sandy began winning. By 1961, he was the best pitcher in baseball.

The day Sandy became a great pitcher was August 31, 1959. On that day, he struck out 18 members of the San Francisco Giants tying the record of Bobby Feller.

White struck out while sitting on the bench.

Sammy White of the Boston Red Sox was sitting comfortably on his team's bench on June 2, 1952 when he struck out. Did he have a 60-foot-long bat? Nope, just the victim of a strange rule.

White was facing the Chicago White Sox when manager Lou Boudreau made his move. White had a count of no balls and two strikes on him when he was called back from the plate. Boudreau had decided to change his strategy, and go with a pinch hitter.

The pinch hitter, Walt Dropo, took a ball, fouled another off, and then swung and missed on the next pitch.

Under the rules of that day, the time at bat—and the strikeout—were charged to White, even though he was sitting quietly on the bench when the K was marked against his name.

What a turnaround!

In 1968, the New York Mets won 73 games, lost 89, had a .451 percentage, and finished in ninth place!

The next season, in 1969, they managed to win 100 games, lost only 62, and they picked up 27 games, a pennant, and a world championship.

Jackson hit 408 in 1911, and didn't win the batting championship.

In 1911, Shoeless Joe Jackson of the Cleveland Indians batted .408, yet lost the batting title by 12 points. He had the bad luck to hit over .400 the year Ty Cobb decided to hit .420. This is a record for the highest batting average by a loser, a mark not likely to be equalled.

Berra caught 148 games without an error.

Yogi Berra was famed for his great bat, but it is also important to remember— the Yankees certainly do—that old Yogi was pretty good with the glove, too.

Between July 28, 1957 and May 10, 1959, Yogi caught 148 games for the Yanks without a single error. Nobody could say Yogi Berra was just another pretty face.

Adcock was a Dodger-killer.

In 1956, Brooklyn Dodger pitchers ran for cover when Joe Adcock, the big first baseman of the Milwaukee Braves, came to bat. On no less than 13 occasions, Adcock hit homers against the Dodgers.

The fact is, he hit 38 homers that year, so he just wasn't picking on the Dodgers.

Haddix pitched 11 perfect innings, and lost the game.

Harvey Haddix, a smallish lefthander for the Pittsburgh Pirates, was starting against the Milwaukee Braves on May 26, 1959. If he had known what was going to happen to him, he would have stayed in bed.

Haddix went through nine perfect innings. He did not allow a single batter to get on base. Yet, while Haddix was knocking off the Braves as fast as they came to the plate, his teammates couldn't squeeze out a single run. At the end of nine innings, it was a scoreless tie. The same for 10 innings; the same for 11.

In the 12th inning, Haddix finally allowed a walk to break up his perfect game. This was followed by an error.

Then Joe Adcock hit a home run, but the first runner, Johnny Logan, was passed by the second runner, Hank Aaron, and the score reverted to 1-0. It was a confusing game for the official scorer, and a depressing one for Harvey Haddix. After 11 perfect innings, he lost the game.

Home-Run Baker shows the way.

Why would a man with no more than 12 homers in any season be called Home-Run anything?

Frank Baker earned the nickname Home-Run Baker in a very simple way. First of all, he led the American League in home runs four straight years in the dead ball era with 9, 10, 12, and 8.

He gained much of his fame in the 1911 World Series when he slammed consecutive home runs in two games off Rube Marquard, considered the best lefthander in the game, and Christy Mathewson, considered the best righthander in the game.

Each day he hit a home run, his name would appear in huge signs across the country where the World Series scores were posted, in the days before radio and television. The signs would give the score and then say, "Home run, Baker." After a couple of days of that, people simply began calling the slugging third baseman Home-Run Baker.

It was eight years later that Babe Ruth hit 29 homers to break Baker's mark. Then the Babe went on to seasons of 54, 59, and 60.

The Indians got nine straight hits and nine straight runs in one inning.

The Cleveland Indians really picked on the Boston Red Sox in a game on June 8, 1908. In the fifth inning of that no-contest, the Indians send nine men to the plate. They got nine straight hits, and they scored nine straight runs.

The Red Sox were so shocked by that performance, they went on to lose seven games in a row.

Beating the best.

On April 23, 1952, Bobby Cain of the St. Louis Browns outpitched Bob Feller of the Cleveland Indians in a tremendous pitchers' battle.

Feller allowed only one hit, a triple, as he recorded his 11th career one hitter. He won the game, right? Wrong! Wrong! Wrong!

That run scored on a sacrifice fly. While all this was going on, Cain allowed only one single and the Indians couldn't move the runner.

The final score was 1-0 for the Browns. The two hits were the lowest number ever recorded in an American League game.

They were hitless, but they weren't winless.

There have been a lot of ball players known as hitless wonders, but only one team deserved the name.

That was the Chicago White Sox of 1906 who batted .230 as a team with the highest average hitter, Frank Isbell, the second baseman batting .279. Six of the nine regulars batted under .250, with third baseman, Lee Tannehill, batting all of .183.

A team that poor in hitting figured to finish at the bottom of the league. Not so with the Chicago White Sox of 1906, the Hitless Wonders of the world.

The White Sox won the pennant. Then they beat the famed Chicago Cubs 4-2 in the World Series, proving once again, it's not how hard you hit the ball or how often, but how well you play the game.

Score one for the Indians.

In 1955, the Indians came up with a lefthanded pitcher by the name of Herb Score. He went through the American League hitters like they were all minor leaguers. Score whiffed 245 batters that season—a record for rookies.

Score's future seemed unlimited. He won 16 games as a rookie, and then 20 the next year.

In 1957, Score was hit by a line drive in the eye off the bat of Gil McDougald of the Yankees. For a time, his life was threatened.

Herb was well enough to pitch the following season, but he was never a good pitcher again. A pity, because he might have been one of the best.

A foggy day in New York town.

Everything seemed to happen in Brooklyn before the Dodgers moved west to Los Angeles. One of the wildest events occurred on June 6, 1957, the last year the Dodgers were in Brooklyn.

On that day, after a heavy rain, the field was covered with fog. Nobody could see their fingers in front of them. Fly balls were dropped in the first inning, because the players couldn't find them in the dense atmosphere!

After an inning of this, the umpires wised up. They called time, hoping the fog would lift. The only thing to be lifted were a few wallets as fans groped their way to the food stands to wait it all out.

Finally, the umpires yelled, "No game today, called on account of fog."

Mack managed the A's when he was 88.

In 1950, Connie Mack was managing the Philadelphia A's. He was 88 years old, by far the oldest manager in baseball history. What was the secret of his success?

Well, for one thing, he was a very fine manager with nine pennants in 50 years.

For another thing, he owned the club. When a manager owns a club, the chances are he will hang around as long as his money holds up.

A roller coaster hitter.

Roy Campanella, the Hall of Fame catcher of the Brooklyn Dodgers, had one of the most up and down careers in baseball history—some of the best seasons, and some of the worst.

In 1951, he batted .325 with 108 RBIs and 33 home runs.

The next year he batted only .269, but had 97 RBIs and 22 homers.

In 1953, he led the league with 142 RBIs, batted .312, and had 41 homers as he crashed the walls at Ebbets Field. Now he was ready to start breaking home run records.

Not so fast. Campy then had an injury-filled year, batted a low of .207, had only 51 RBIs, and 19 homers.

All in all, a hard man to figure for a good year or a bad year.

Home run city.

Philadelphia Shibe Park was the scene of one of the wildest games in baseball history.

On July 10, 1929, Philadelphia and Pittsburgh played a game won by the Pirates 9-7. There were 27 hits in the game and nine homers—four by the Pirates and five by the Phillies—a home run in every inning, except one. The game lasted three hours and 14 minutes.

Mantle hit a 565-foot home run.

Long home runs have been a Yankee tradition from Babe Ruth and Lou Gehrig through Joe DiMaggio and Charlie Keller.

The longest homer ever hit came on April 17, 1953 in Washington. Mickey Mantle was the batter, Chuck Stobbs pitching for Washington.

Stobbs, a lefthander, threw a fastball and Mantle caught it on the fat part of the bat. The ball took off like a rocket.

It sailed and sailed and sailed, over the fence and beyond the street in Griffith Stadium. The Yankee publicity director, Red Patterson, ran outside the park with a tape measure, asked some kids where it had landed, and then measured the distance.

The ball had stopped 565 feet from home plate, a Herculean wallop, the longest recorded homer in Yankee history, and probably, in all baseball.

Wonderful Willie Mays shows the way to Wertz.

"You can shake a tree, and a dozen fielders will fall out," Branch Rickey once said. He meant that a lot of baseball players were good from the defensive point of the game, but only some rare ones were good on the offense, and only the great ones could do it all: run, hit, field, throw, and catch the ball with equal skill. Willie Mays was one of the rarest.

Mays had been a sensational rookie center fielder for the Giants in the 1951 season. He had broken in with an 0-12 in three games in Philadelphia. Manager Leo Durocher put his arm around the young center fielder, told him to stop worrying about his hitting and said, "You're my center fielder no matter what happens."

Durocher knew that even if Mays hit .000—perish the thought—Willie's defensive genius would still be valuable to the Giants. Leo was never more correct than on September 29, 1954, when the Giants played the Cleveland Indians in the first game of the World Series. Cleveland had had a marvelous season. They had won 111 games, defeated Casey Stengel's Yankees by eight games, and were considered to be one of the great teams of all time. Their pitching staff included Bob Lemon, Early Wynn, Mike Garcia, and Bob Feller.

The first game was tied 2-2 in the eighth inning with Lemon battling Sal Maglie. The Indians got two on in the eighth, and Vic Wertz was at the plate. The pitcher was now Don Liddle for the Giants, in relief of Maglie. A hit would win the game. That's the way the script was written.

No script ever was more wrong. Wertz connected against Liddle, and drove the ball on a high arch toward the center field bleachers some 505 feet away from home plate. But Mays raced back, back, back, leaped into the air like a ballet dancer and plucked the ball from the sky.

The runners had almost gotten home when they were shocked by the catch, and raced back just in time to avoid getting doubled up. It was the greatest fielding play anyone could remember in World Series history.

"How do you rate it with some other catches you have made," Mays was asked. Said the young man from Alabama, "I don't rate 'em, I just catch 'em."

And how!

Charley Hustle shows them why.

For years, he had been known as Charley Hustle, a name tagged on him by Whitey Ford of the Yankees.

"Go get 'em, Charley Hustle," yelled Ford, not knowing that he would be tagging Pete Rose with a name that would stay with him throughout his career. Rose would, years later, wear a T-shirt reading, "Hustle makes it happen."

On the artificial turf at Riverfront Stadium in Cincinnati on July 14, 1970, Rose would show the world why.

The National league and the American League were engaged in a bitter All-Star game battle. They were tied 4-4, in the bottom of the 12th inning. The crowd of 51,838 was getting its money's worth as the game went into extra innings.

There were two out and nobody on base as Clyde Wright of the California Angels pitched to Pete Rose. The stocky Reds' outfielder smashed a hard single to left field, and the National League had the potential winning run on first base.

Then Billy Grabarkewitz of the Los Angeles Dodgers smacked another single on the ground to left field and Rose was on second.

Jim Hickman of the Cubs was the batter as Wright took his sign from Ray Fosse of the Cleveland Indians. Fosse had spent the previous evening with Rose and several Cincinnati teammates, having dinner together, talking about the coming game, and enjoying the sights.

Now came the pitch to Hickman. Boom! A line drive that jumped off his bat like a scared rabbit in the woods. Rose, not particularly a fast runner— but a tough one—raced around third base. It seemed as if he would be out easily as the throw to home plate got there ahead of him. But this was Charley Hustle one must remember, and he didn't give up easily. He slid with full force into Fosse, knocked the catcher over, and sprawled in the dirt with the winning run.

"Am I safe?" he asked the umpire, Al Barlick, at home plate, before being helped off the field.

Fosse was knocked for a loop and never again was the player he had been.

Rose had hustled home with a run that meant the game. "Did you hurt yourself on that slide?" he was asked afterwards. "We won, didn't we?" he replied. To Charley Hustle, that was all that counted.

The ultimate pitchers' duel.

Anything you can do, I can do better—that's what Cincinnati pitcher Fred Toney seemed to be saying to his mound rival, Hippo Vaughn of Chicago. Inning after inning, Vaughn set down the Reds without a hit. Inning after inning, Toney treated the Cubs with similar disdain. On this second day of May, 1917, the 3,500 fans in Chicago's Weeghman Park were being treated to a pitchers' duel without parallel.

In the top of the ninth, the lefthanded Vaughn set down the Reds to complete his no-hitter. What he needed now was a run. But the Cubs still couldn't get a hit, as Toney completed *his* no-hitter.

In the top of the tenth, Red shortstop Larry Kopf drove a clean single to right, and after an error sent Kopf to third, Jim Thorpe hit a swinging roller down the third-base line. Vaughn had no play to first on the speedy Olympic hero, so he threw home to try to catch Kopf. But the Cub catcher, Art Wilson, was looking off toward first base, expecting Vaughn's throw to go there. When Hippo's throw arrived at the plate, it hit Wilson smack in the chest, and the run was in.

Toney had no trouble retiring the demoralized Cubs, and won his no-hitter. After losing the heartbreaker, all Vaughn could say in the clubhouse was, "Well, it's just another game."

But it wasn't. There had never been another to match it.

Hoyt puts a halt to Yankees.

Hoyt Wilhelm, a distinguished knuckleball pitcher, has two anti-Yankee records that will not be forgotten. On September 20, 1961, Wilhelm faced Roger Maris of the Yankees in Baltimore Stadium. Maris had a home run record on the line.

The great player had hit homer number 59 of the season that night against Milt Pappas. Maris was shooting to tie Babe Ruth's 60 homers in 154 games, even though the 1961 season was 162 games. The pressure was on Maris.

Wilhelm threw one of his fancy, dancin' knuckleballs and Maris topped the ball to the mound. He was out, and the Babe's 154-game mark was safe even though Maris did hit 61 in 162 games that year.

Who's last?

Need a guide around baseball's cellar?

Then Philadelphia's the place to go. Totaled together, the two teams of the City of Brotherly Love had wound up in the last place 42 times by 1973. Each club holds the all-time record for finishing last in its league.

How fleeting is fame!

One of the strangest careers in the history of professional baseball is that of Joseph E. Borden. In 1875, he pitched for the Philadelphia Athletics under the pseudonym of Joseph E. Josephs. Although his record that year was a mere two wins against four losses, one of his victories was a no-hitter, the very first on record.

The next year was marked by the formation of the National League. On April 22, 1876, the first game in National League history was played in Philadelphia, with the Boston Red Stockings nipping the Athletics, 6-5. The winning pitcher? Joe Borden, by now pitching in Beantown under his own name.

A month and a day later, Borden threw another no-hitter, this one the first in National League history.

But with all these first, Borden managed to compile a won-lost record of only 12-12 in 1876. Before the season was over, he was given his walking papers by the brass, and finished the year as the grounds-keeper of the Boston ballpark. Joe Borden was then only 22, but he never pitched another big-league game.

Baseball's first great pitcher.

In 1870, Rockford defeated the mighty Cincinnati Red Stockings, managed by Harry Wright. The winning hurler was a 20-year-old youth by the name of Albert Goodwill Spalding.

When Wright left Cincinnati the next year to organize a new team in Boston, he invited Spalding to join him: And it was in Beantown that Spalding had his greatest years. After winning 21 games in 1871, over the next four years he went on to post records of 36-8, 41-15, 52-18, and 56-5!

In 1876, Spalding was not quite 26 years old, yet he was signed to manage the Chicago White Stockings. Spalding led his team to the pennant, winning 46 games himself.

Three years later, Spalding retired from active play, and went on to make a fortune in the sporting goods firm which still bears his name today.

Fanned in Boston.

Dizzy Dean was never hesitant about putting his money where his mouth was—and with ol' Diz's mouth, that's saying a lot.

Diz had a friend named Johnny Perkins who worked in a St. Louis nightclub, and occasionally Perkins followed the Cards on their road trips. On the train up to Boston early in 1937, Perkins bet Diz that he couldn't strike out the Bees' rookie Vince DiMaggio the first time he came up.

Dean did manage to fan DiMaggio, and from the bench, Dizzy signaled to Perkins that he'd go double or nothing on Vince's next time up. Perkins agreed, and again Dean won the bet.

The same wager held on DiMaggio's third trip, and once again Dean took more of Perkins' money and DiMaggio's pride. As Vince came to the plate for the fourth time, he had no idea that he was a pawn in this game of high finance. He bore down and at last got a piece of the ball, lifting a high foul pop in back of the plate.

Diz ran toward home screaming at his catcher, Bob Ogrodowski, "Let it go, let it go!" Fortunately for Dean, the ball hit the screen on its downward arc, and the catcher couldn't lay his mitt on it for a putout. Then Diz went back to the mound and fanned DiMaggio for the fourth straight time.

The kid hits a big one.

It had always been an exhibition of the best against the best, the All-Star game, a creation of a newspaperman. It was Arch Ward of the Chicago Tribune who dreamed the impossible dream of putting the best of each league against each other in a summer classic.

Babe Ruth had hit a home run in the first game in 1933, and the idea had caught on big. In 1941, as war approached, fans realized many of the players would be away in service for many years. So Ted Williams—The Kid—gave them something to remember.

The National League led the Americans 5-4 with two out, two on, and Ted Williams up. Williams was on his way to a .406 season, as he came to bat that day in Detroit against Claude Passeau of the Chicago Cubs. Joe DiMaggio had just hit into a forceout; and Passeau, a tricky curve baller, had only to retire Williams to end the game and give the National League a victory.

Passeau worked The Kid carefully and finally threw one down the center of the plate. Like lightning, Williams whipped that thin-handled bat, and drove the baseball high over the roof in right field for a 7-5 American League win.

The blow proved so emotional that manager Del Baker of Detroit, leading the American Leaguers that day, hugged and kissed the grinning Williams at home plate. It was a blow The Kid would never forget. Nor would any of the 54,674 fans who had seen that great clutch smash by a tremendous hitter.

Base-stealing specialist.

When base-stealing specialist Herb Washington was released by the Oakland A's early in the 1975 season, he left behind him one of the most puzzling statistical entries in the baseball record books: 31 stolen bases and not a single appearance at the plate.

Who says 13 is unlucky?

When California's Ed Figueroa stopped Kansas City 6-2, the victory marked the Angels' first win over the Royals in their last 13 meetings in 1975. And what's more, Figueroa finally figured out how to retire third baseman George Brett, who had reached him for 13 straight hits.

The date of this event? September 13.

THE HALL OF BLUNDERS

What a pair of hands.

From 1960 through 1966, Hector Lopez was a journeyman outfielder with the New York Yankees.

Lopez was a good hitter who averaged a creditable .269 for 12 big league seasons. But that's not what he's known for.

One afternoon, the Yankees were playing the Tigers. Norm Cash was up for Detroit and he hit a line drive to right field. The ball shot smack-dab into Lopez's glove.

All of a sudden, the pellet plummeted from the pocket of the glove to the ground for a three-base blunder. The Tigers beat the Yankees that day, and Hector Lopez was known forever after as Hector What-a-Pair-of- Hands Lopez.

Be kind to your Nabors.

Johnny Nabors was a pitcher for the Philadelphia Athletics in 1916. He got into 40 games, started in 29, and managed to lose 19 in a row—a matchless record in futility.

Torre hits four double plays in one game.

On July 21, 1975, Felix Millan of the New York Mets stroked four singles—in the first inning, the third, the sixth, and the eighth. Try as he might, on none of these occasions was he able to reach second. Each time, lumbering Joe Torre erased him by grounding into a double play!

Joe's dubious feat has no parallel in National League annals, but he does have to share "honors" with two American Leaguers: both Goose Goslin of the Senators, in 1934, and Mike Kreevich of the White Sox, in 1939, also hit into four double plays in one game.

Merullo shoulda stood in bed!

On September 13, 1942, Lennie Merullo shoulda stood in bed. On that day, in one troublesome inning, the Cub shortstop accepted four fielding chances and bobbled every one!

Oh! Oh! Oh! Oh!

Boggs hit three batters in a row.

On September 17, 1928, Ray Boggs, pitcher for the Boston Braves, set a record for futility. In a game against the Chicago Cubs, Boggs hit the first man he faced, then the second man, then the third man.

Three batters faced, three batters hit. Fortunately, nobody was hurt but Boggs. Ray got into only four games that year for the Braves, and never again pitched in the Major Leagues.

Marvelous Marv misses them all.

In 1962, before he started to do beer commercials, Marv Throneberry was first baseman for the New York Mets. Or he stood around first, anyway.

One day, the Mets were short of coaches and Marvelous Marv—so called because he wasn't—was not in the game but in the coach's box at first base.

Casey Stengel had used up all of his pinch hitters. He looked down at the first base coaching box and discovered the Marvelous one, and called him in to hit.

With a man on first base, Marvelous came to the plate. He caught the first pitch right on the button, and drove in into a gap in right center field. Around first he went, around second he went, and into third in a cloud of dust for a triple.

Or so it seemed. Suddenly the fielders were relaying the ball to first and the umpire was calling Marv out.

"Out, how could he be out?" yelled manager Stengel.

"He missed first base," said the umpire.

Stengel continued to argue. Finally, he gave up and started walking off the field.

"There's really no use arguing," said third base coach, Cookie Lavagetto. "He also missed second."

In a strikeout class by himself.

Bobby Bonds is the Babe Ruth of strikeouts. He once struck out 189 times in 663 at bats for the San Francisco Giants, a ratio of nearly one strikeout every three times at the plate. Bonds hit .302 that year with 26 homers.

Kindall stirs up the breeze.

In nine years with the Cubs, the Indians, and the Twins, Jerry Kindall had a lifetime batting average of .213. Nobody could accuse him of being a good hitter.

On August 14, 1960, he was a ridiculous hitter. Kindall was playing second base for the Cubs, when he batted against Dallas Green of the Phillies. He hit a ground ball his first time up, and then struck out three times in a row.

The Cubs were off the next day.

On the 16th, the Cubs went against the Cards. Kindall faced four different pitchers as the Cubs knocked the Redbirds around. Kindall had struck out seven straight times in the two games!

Ron Swoboda struck out five times in one day.

The New York Mets were playing a doubleheader against the St. Louis Cardinals. Ron Swoboda, a young outfielder, came up eight times in the doubleheader, and went down five times on strikes.

Somehow, the Mets managed to win one of the two games.

"It's a good thing we did," said Swoboda. "If we'd lost both games, I'd be eating my heart out. As it is, I'm only eating out one ventricle."

Lisenbee yielded 26 hits and 13 runs in one game.

Horace Lisenbee, "Hod" to baseball people, won 18 games and lost nine in 1927 for the Washington Senators. He lived off that year for the rest of his career, every team and every manager waiting for him to repeat.

On September 11, 1936, after putting together six losing seasons, Hod Lisenbee, pitching for the Philadelphia A's, faced the Yankees. The Bronx Bombers has already clinched the pennant in Joe DiMaggio's rookie season with the club.

Philadelphia was heading nowhere, except for the American League basement, and had a depleted staff. So Connie Mack told Lisenbee, "You're my pitcher today." He was also the Yankee's pitcher. They smacked him around for 13 runs and 26 hits.

Knuckle down, Hoyt.

One of the toughest pitches for a batter to handle is the flutterball or knuckleball, a pitch that dances and dips as it comes to the plate. Hitters and catchers hate it with equal intensity.

In 1958, the best pitcher on the Baltimore Orioles was Hoyt Wilhelm who threw knuckleballs 98 percent of the time. The other two percent of the time, he threw fastballs that looked like knuckleballs.

His catcher, Gus Triandos, was almost driven nuts by Wilhelm's knuckleball. Forty-six passed balls got by Gus that season, for a record that is likely to stand as long as baseball is played.

It must have been slippery elm.

In 1960, National League pitchers accounted for 310 wild pitches, a record for inaccuracy that hasn't been touched.

Catchers were chasing all over the place with many of them believing their pitchers were doing it to them on purpose.

The A's lost 20 games in a row— on two different occasions.

In 1916, the A's power-dived into the American League cellar by losing 20 games in a row. Just to show it wasn't a freak, the A's repeated in 1943, again hitting the skids for 20 successive losses.

Connie Mack surely learned how to take it.

What's in a name?

The man with the longest name in baseball history, was Calvin Coolidge Julius Caesar Tuskahoma (Buster) McLish, who pitched for the Cleveland Indians in 1956.

On May 27, 1956, he faced the powerful Boston Red Sox. Ted Williams was the first batter up. He homered. Then came Frank Malzone, and he homered. Them came Gene Mauch, a weakling at the plate, but he also homered. Then came Dick Gernert—and he homered.

Yes, Buster McLish surely made a record for himself.

Joe Torre needs a shortstop to call his own.

In 1975, on July 21, Joe Torre batted four times, hit four ground balls, and accounted for eight outs. On that day, unlucky Joe hit into four double plays in a row.

Goslin hit into four double plays in one afternoon.

On April 28, 1934, you could fry an egg on the head of manager Mickey Cochrane, after he witnessed the performance of outfielder Goose Goslin.

The Detroit outfielder had four at bats that day and hit into four double plays in a row.

As if that wasn't bad enough, on his only chance in the outfield, Goslin managed to drop a fly ball that allowed in the only run for Cleveland.

Fortunately for the Goose, Detroit was still able to win the game 4-1.

Charlie Neal starts the season with a bang.

The New York Mets won 40 games and lost 120 in 1962.

They were hoping the 1963 season would be a little better as they opened play in the Polo Grounds against the Cardinals.

The first batter for St. Louis was center fielder Curt Flood. Flood hit a routine ground ball to third that your aunt Nellie could have fielded. Sure enough, Charles Neal, the third baseman of the Mets, fielded it like your aunt Nellie. He picked up the ball smoothly, and then fired it smartly into right field as Flood raced to third.

Pitching debut.

On June 23, 1915, Bruno P. Haas made what is probably the most inauspicious pitching debut in big league annals.

A schoolboy fresh from Worcester Academy, Haas was pitching for the Athletics against the Yanks. In nine raucous innings, Haas yielded 16 bases on balls—a major league record. To make his parents even more proud, Bruno unleased three wild pitches. His teammates soon caught the spirit of the day and contributed six errors to the afternoon's fun.

The Yanks spent a pleasant June afternoon strolling around the bases. The scorekeeper counted 15 tallies.

Maranville was caught stealing— three times in one game.

Walter James Vincent Maranville was 5 feet, 5 inches tall, weighed 155 pounds, and was known as "The Rabbit" during his long career with the Braves, the Pirates, the Cubs, the Dodgers, and the Cardinals.

Maranville was fast, but he wasn't so fast that they couldn't get him.

On June 6, 1913, Maranville, playing for Boston, tried to steal three times against the Cubs, and three times, catcher Jimmy Archer nailed him, just as if "The Rabbit" were standing still.

Ryan struck out 383 in one season.

American League batters could hardly be blamed if they called in sick any time they had to face Nolan Ryan in 1973.

The young man with the 104-mile-per-hour fastball was really throwing smoke that season. Called *Ryan's Express*, his fastball was making hitters whiff ingloriously as he blazed past them, again and again.

Bobby Feller of the Cleveland Indians had set a strikeout record in 1946, when he struck out 348.

In 1965, Sandy Koufax, of the Los Angeles Dodgers, blew away 382 National League batters for a new mark.

Along came *Ryan's Express* and the record was shattered. On the final day of the season, Ryan managed to record strikeout number 383, even though he could barely lift his right arm above his knees.

Ryan continued to be the most feared strikeout pitcher in all baseball history.

George shoulda had a twin.

During the years 1966, 1974, and 1975, George Scott of the Boston Red Sox specialized in double plays. In each of those seasons, George hit into more double plays than any hitter in the league. However, in 1954, Jackie Jensen of the Red Sox smacked into 32 twin killings—a record not to be proud of, but still a record.

ANECDOTES OF THE BIG—TIME

Grooving one at the wrong time.

On June 14, 1965, Jim Maloney, of the Cincinnati Reds, was facing the New York Mets. Suddenly, Maloney was in the 11th inning with a no-hitter. He hadn't allowed a single hit, but his teammates hadn't produced either.

It was 0-0 as Johnny Lewis came up in the 11th for the Mets. There was a man on second via a walk and a sacrifice bunt. Lewis looked at one pitch, and then smacked the next into right field for the first hit and the first run of the game.

Maloney wound up losing 1-0.

Hank gets the wrong guy on the wrong day.

Hank Greenberg of the Detroit Tigers— one of the great sluggers of all time—had 58 home runs on the last day of the 1938 season. He was driving hard on Babe Ruth's mark of 60 homers in a single season.

Greenberg wanted two homers that day to tie the Babe, but ran into Cleveland's Bobby Feller.

In those days, Feller was the best pitcher in the business, and on that day he was smoking. He struck out 18 members of the Tigers, and Greenberg never got his homers.

The sit-down strike.

On May 15, 1912, the Detroit Tigers were playing the New York Yankees at the Polo Grounds. Ty Cobb was being heckled incessantly by one fan in the grandstand, and as the game wore on, the Georgia Peach's patience wore exceedingly thin. He asked the New York manager to do something, since crowd control was the responsibility of the home team. But this particular fan continued to malign Cobb's play, his lineage, and his manhood.

At last, not able to listen to another word of abuse, Cobb leapt into the stands and began to furiously pummel his tormentor. By the time police and spectators intervened, the erstwhile heckler was a bruised and bloody mess.

American League President Ban Johnson read the umpires' report of the incident, fined Cobb $100, and suspended him for 10 days. Although Cobb was perhaps the least-liked man in baseball—even by his teammates—the Tiger players rallied to his support. Either Cobb played, the Tigers said, or they didn't.

Johnson ignored this threat and forced a showdown. The Tigers were due to play the Athletics in Philadelphia on May 18. If Detroit could not field a team on that date, Johnson said, they would have to pay a $5,000 fine to the league.

Detroit Manager Hughie Jennings pleaded with his men, but to no avail. They would not play without Cobb. On the morning of the game with the A's, Jennings signed up nine youths from St. Joseph's College and the Philadelphia sandlots—Bill Leinhauser, Dan McGarvey, Billy Maharg, Jim McGarr, Pat Meany, Jack Coffey, Hap Ward, Ed Irwin, and Aloysius Travers. All nine recruits played that afternoon, aided by two fortyish Tiger coaches who returned to active duty for the day.

The game was a horror, as pitcher Travers was belted for 24 runs. It wasn't all his fault, though, because nine errors by his teammates led to 10 unearned runs. The fans who paid to see this game may have been bilked, but the Tiger management had saved itself five grand.

At Cobb's behest, the regular Tigers returned to the field the next day. The nine instant major leaguers were paid and released. Only one ever donned a major league uniform again: Billy Maharg, who four years later made another one-day stand, this time with the Phillies.

Strangely, nothing was ever heard again of Ed Irwin, who was the Tiger catcher on the day of the strike. He belted out two triples in three times at bat, and thus ended his big league career with a batting average of .667.

A grand beginning with a big breeze.

The Detroit Tigers were marching toward a pennant in 1968, when their lefthander John Hiller took the mound against the Minnesota Twins. It was August 6, 1968.

In the first inning, Hiller retired three straight batters on strikes. The crowd roared as he walked off the field. Then came the second inning. Another strikeout. Then another. Then a third.

Six batters, straight, all striking out against Hiller's flaming fastball. Hiller got two strikes on the next hitter, then a soft fly ball was wafted to Al Kaline in right field. Hiller's streak was over.

Three other pitchers since Hiller have started games with six straight strikeouts—Ray Culp for Boston in 1970, Bert Blyleven for Minnesota in 1970, and Andy Messersmith for the Dodgers in 1973.

He had the big guy's number.

Hub Pruett was a soft-throwing journeyman lefthanded pitcher with the St. Louis Browns for three season. Then he moved over to the National League.

Pruett was able to win only 14 American League games in his entire career; so he isn't known for his wins. However, he is known for the way he tortured the Babe.

At the peak of his career, Ruth came to bat 31 times against Pruett, and struck out against him 19 times. The Babe was never able to get a home run off the thin lefthander from Malden, Missouri, and the big guy was thrilled when Pruett was traded to the Phillies in 1927.

Babe celebrated Pruett's absence in the league by having the best year of his life with 60 homers.

It ain't nothing 'til I call it.

That was the creed of umpire Bill Klem. He had a right to be a little independent about his umpiring skill. He had been around for quite some while.

Klem umpired his first big league game in 1905, and monitored his last in 1941.

According to Klem, in all those years he never missed a call.

It's the real thing, or the rub that refreshes.

Guy Bush, a first-rate pitcher for the Cubs for more than a decade, once came to his trainer and asked what could be done for his sore arm. The trainer, Andy Lotshaw, rubbed up Bush's aching right arm with his secret liniment, and sent Bush on his way. Bush won.

By the time his next turn rolled around, Bush's arm was feeling much better, thank you, but he thought he'd take a little liniment just to be safe. He won again. This ritual continued for years; Bush swore by Lotshaw's secret cure.

When Bush finally retired, Lotshaw revealed the secret behind his secret cure. On that first day, when Bush had complained of a sore arm, Lotshaw had reached into his kit for liniment only to find he was all out. Thinking that Bush's ailment was located above the neck, the trainer reached for the first bottle of liquid he could lay his hands on. It was a bottle of Coca-Cola. And it was Coca-Cola that Lotshaw continued to rub on Bush's arm for the rest of his days with the Cubs.

The Babe makes a booboo.

On October 10, 1926, one of the strangest plays in baseball history occurred in the World Series between the New York Yankees and the St. Louis Cardinals.

The Series was tied three games each, when the 7th game began at Yankee Stadium. The Cardinals were holding a shaky 3-2 lead in the ninth inning.

"Old Pete," Grover Cleveland Alexander, had held the Yankees off in relief. Now it was two out in the bottom of the 9th. Alexander worked carefully on Babe Ruth and finally walked him. He was the tying run, with Bob Meusel up next. Lou Gehrig would follow.

All of a sudden, Babe shocked the fans, his manager, and the crowd by taking off on a steal of second base. The one guy he didn't shock—and the most important of all—was St. Louis catcher Bob O'Farrell. He fired the ball down to second and The Babe was out in a cloud of dust. The game was over, the Series was over, and Meusel and Gehrig were left at the plate without a swing. All Babe got out of his attempted steal was a lot of egg on his face.

Rocky Swoboda lets loose with a caper.

The Mets were playing the St. Louis Cardinals one day. Larry Bearnarth was pitching for the Mets with a 3-0 lead. There were two men out, and there were three men on.

Dal Maxvill of the Cards hit a routine fly ball to right on that cloudy day. As the ball sailed to right field, the sun broke through the haze. Rocky Swoboda, who hardly ever needed an excuse for missing a fly ball, lost this one in the sun. The ball fell behind him and three runners scored to tie the game.

As luck would have it, Swoboda was the leadoff hitter the next inning. He came to bat and was struck out on three straight pitches.

He was so angry that he threw his helmet down on the dugout step, stomped on it, cutting into it with his spikes. The helmet stuck to his shoe like chewing gum.

"Get into the clubhouse," screamed manager Casey Stengel. "I'm gonna go inside and step on your watch."

Swoboda was embarrassed. He walked quietly inside.

"If everybody on this team commenced breaking up the furniture every time we did bad," growled Stengel, "there'd be no place to sit."

Big, big hitters, but no winners.

The Cincinnati Reds of 1956 and the New York Giants of 1947 share an interesting record. The Reds and Giants each hit 221 homers in those particular seasons. But the Giants of 1947 finished in fourth place, and the Reds of 1956 finished in third place, proving once again that baseball teams do not live by home runs alone.

Steve Carlton lets two get away.

One of the greatest pitching performances in baseball history was ruined by a couple of pitching blunders by lefthander Steve Carlton of the Cardinals.

On September 15, 1969, Carlton was firing bullets at the New York Mets. He was striking them out at a rate of more than two per inning. He would end the game with 19 strikeouts, a record for a nine-inning game.

Carlton would make a couple of blunders along the way. He grooved two fastballs. Each time he did, Ron Swoboda hit the ball out of the park.

But the Cards were only able to score three runs; so Swoboda's two homers—each with a man on base—gave the Mets a surprising 4-3 victory.

Bobo Newsom was the most travelin' man.

In 20 years in the big leagues, Bobo Newsom must have paid more fare than any other player in the history of the game. He was traded 13 different times to eight different teams, coming home to Washington on no less than four occasions.

Say it ain't so, Joe.

Joe Torre, the catcher for the St. Louis Cardinals, was at bat in a game against the Mets at Shea Stadium. He lined a ball to right field for a hit, and tried to stretch it into a double. The right fielder fired the ball to second, and the slow running Torre was out by a mile.

Umpire Tom Gorman stood over the play, watched Torre slide, watched the shortstop make the tag and bellowed, "Y'er out!"

Torre lay on the ground smiling.

"I can't be out," he said, "the ball rolled off the fielder's glove and is in my shirt."

Gorman studied the situation as the dust cleared.

"You know that," the umpire said, "and the shortstop knows that, but 50,000 people just saw me call you out, *so you're out!*"

And he was.

Opening a season with a bang.

Bob Feller of the Cleveland Indians was the starting pitcher on opening day in 1940 against the Chicago White Sox in Comiskey Park.

He pitched a no-hit, no-run game against the White Sox, but some of the joy of the afternoon was taken away from Feller by a strange accident.

On one of Bob's serves to the plate, the batter hit a foul ball which struck Bobby Feller's mother, who was sitting in the stands. The injury proved not to be serious. But for awhile, Feller was more concerned about his mother's eye than he was about his no-hitter.

A hard man to whiff.

Joe Sewell of the Cleveland Indians batted 608 times in 1925, and was up 578 times in 1928. The only thing those two seasons had in common was Sewell's strikeout total. In each season, American League pitchers were only able to get wary little Joe only four times on strikes.

Lose them all, lose them all.

In 1937, Hugh Mulcahy of the Phillies had a record of eight wins and 18 losses.

In 1938, he was 10-20.

In 1939, he was 9-16.

In 1940, he was 13-22.

Philadephia sportswriters, never known for their kindness toward members of the Phillies, decided they would brand the pitcher with a name he had earned through the years. As the Western Union ticker gave the scores, it also listed the pitcher. It became a standard thing to see next to a Phillies game, the name Loser-Mulcahy. The sportwriters soon made it part of his name, and they always referred to the big right-hander as Loser Mulcahy.

Finally, Loser Mulcahy could take it no more. He ran away from the Phillies and joined the Army. He thought he would take a year away from baseball in 1941, and then improve his record.

Loser Mulcahy was true to his name. Just as soon as he got into the Army, World War II broke out, and Loser Mulcahy, the first big leaguer in service in World War II, became one of the last to get out.

What to do in St. Petersburg, Florida.

St. Petersburg, Florida, where the Yankees customarily reside during spring training, is well known as a haven for pensioners. One spring, after his perfect game in the World Series, pitcher Don Larsen made the local papers by wrapping his new car around a lamppost at 5 A.M. Yankee manager Casey Stengel was asked if he planned to fine Larsen.

"Anybody who can find something to do in St. Petersburg at five in the morning," Casey quipped, "deserves a medal, not a fine."

Spicy spitter.

The last of the spitball pitchers has allegedly vanished from the major leagues, and the saliva delivery is now banned by the rules. But in the spitballer's heyday, the unpredictable behavior of the moistened pitch had many a batter gnashing his teeth. Fred Luderus, first sacker of the Phillies, found one answer to the problem. He fought water with fire!

It was in a 1912 game against the Pirates' Marty O'Toole, a very effective spitball pitcher. O'Toole's moistening technique was to hold the ball up to his face and lick it directly with his tongue. Then he would wind up and send the dampened pill on its eccentric course to the plate.

When the Phillies took the field, Luderus carried in his back pocket a tube of liniment. Every time the ball came his way, the first baseman would rub a little of the fiery ointment into the horsehide. (In those days, a single ball might stay in play for a full nine innings.) Before the third inning was over, O'Toole's tongue was so raw and inflamed he had to be taken out of the box.

Manager Fred Clarke of the Pirates squawked to high heaven. He protested that the use of the liniment was illegal, a threat to eyesight, peace of mind, and the constitution.

But Charlie Dooin, Phillie manager, indignantly rejected Clarke's protests. "I ordered Luderus to do it to protect my boys," he proclaimed self-righteously. "Why, that nasty habit of O'Toole's was putting millions of germs on every pitch."

"And," he concluded, "every time O'Toole spits on that ball, we're going to disinfect it. There's nothing in the rules that says we don't have the right to protect our health!"

And there isn't!

Don't ask.

Luke Appling was one of the greatest shortstops in American League history. He played from 1930 through 1950 with the Chicago White Sox. His lifetime average was .310. He was a brilliant fielder, one of the best Hall of Fame infielders of all time.

There was only one problem with Luke. He was a hypochondriac. He imagined he was heir to every injury known to man, and to every disease. Known as "Old Aches and Pains," he was seriously injured only once in his 20-year career.

When Appling was around, the real blunder was to ask him, "How do you feel?" It would sometimes take half an hour before he stopped telling you.

Pumpsie keeps his secret.

From 1959 to 1962, the Boston Red Sox had an infielder by the name of Pumpsie Green.

Green was often asked how had he acquired such a terrific nickname as Pumpsie. His given name was Elijah Jerry Green.

"A million people have asked me that," he said. "I'm going to write a book next year, and I'll sell it for a dollar to everybody who asks and I'll make a million."

The next year, he was dumped into the minors. Then, nobody asked and nobody cared.

Lucky number 7.

The most hits a team can get in one inning without scoring is 6. How could that be?

It could be like this: Jones singles and is out stretching. Sorry about that, Jones. Smith singles and is out stretching. Nice arm, Brown. Two out, nobody on.

The next three hitters each single. Bases loaded, two out, nobody has scored.

Then here comes the next hitter. He drives a hard ground ball between first and second base. Whoops, it hits the runner. Base runner is declared out. Batter is credited with a single.

Six singles, three outs, no runs, and a manager going nuts.

Top credentials.

At the conclusion of a disappointing 1975, Atlanta Braves' general manager Eddie Robinson stated that he was seeking a "fiery, enthusiastic" type for his next field manager. Later that month, he called a press conference to announce the hiring of Dave Bristol, former manager of the Cincinnati Reds and the Milwaukee Brewers.

One reporter, recalling Robinson's earlier pronouncement, asked Bristol if he were a fiery type.

"I guess so," replied Bristol. "I've been fired three times."

Attendance woes.

In 1975, fans at San Francisco's Candlestick Park were so few and far between that Giant right fielder Bobby Murcer commented, "If they check the upper deck, they might find Patty Hearst hiding out."

Bob Miller finally won one.

On the next to last day of the 1964 season, a righthanded pitcher on the New York Mets by the name of Bob Miller was pitching against the Chicago Cubs. Miller had pitched all year for the Mets without losing a chance at a record— the all-losing record of 12 games without a win.

Russ Miller—no relation to Bob—had lost 12 for the Phillies in 1928 and Steve Gerkin had equalled that number for the A's in 1945.

Miller beat the Cubs 4-2 on the next to last day of the 1964 season and lost his chance for immortality—negative as it is.

Umpire meathead.

Red Jones, an AMerican League umpire in the late 1940s, was being given the business one day by the Chicago bench jockeys. Over and over again, the word "meathead" wafted from the dugout toward home plate. At last, Jones could take no more, and sent everyone on the bench in for an early shower.

The next day, as Jones came out on the field to start the proceedings, he passed in front of the White Sox dugout. "Oh, Mr. Umpire," the players cooed in unison, "you won't have any trouble with us today."

"That's nice," said Red, "but what makes you so sure?"

Then came the chorus: "We can't call you meathead today because it's Friday."

Left at the station.

In 1941, Larry MacPhail was the general manager of the Brooklyn Dodgers. The Dodgers had not won a pennant since 1920, and the fans were hungry for success.

That year, the Dodgers finally clinched the pennant with a victory in Boston.

Baseball teams traveled by train and not by plane in those days, so the Dodgers boarded their train and headed for Grand Central Station in New York.

MacPhail decided to join the train at 125th Street in Manhattan, the last stop before Grand Central. That way he could be on the train with the team, and celebrate the triumph with the waiting fans and newspapermen in Grand Central.

Leo Durocher, the manager of the Dodgers, decided not to allow any of his players to miss the celebration. He ordered the train conductor to pass 125th street without stopping so the entire team—minus GM MacPhail, waiting at the 125th Street station—could celebrate together.

When the train roared through 125th Street, all MacPhail got for his troubles was a face full of train dust and a large share of egg.

All Durocher got for this blunder was a firing.

But, all was forgiven the next day after Durocher explained what had happened.

Would you like to buy the Brooklyn Bridge?

The New York Mets have had a history of making some of the worst trades in the history of the game. Their general managers lead the league in blunders.

For instance, in December of 1969, the Mets traded a young outfielder Amos Otis to the Kansas City Royals for third baseman Joe Foy. Foy batted .236 for the Mets, and was quickly traded away to Washington as a failure.

Otis became an All-Star outfielder for the Royals, batted .281 in the next eight seasons, hit 119 homers, and knocked in 567 runs.

But the best blunder of them all concerned Nolan Ryan who was traded for third baseman Jim Fregosi.

Fregosi hit .232 and .234 for the Mets, while Ryan went on to become one of the great pitchers in the American League with two seasons of 20 wins, and five seasons with more than 300 strikeouts.

The longest Yankee game ever played.

On June 24, 1962, the New York Yankees got into a marathon game in Detroit against the Tigers. It went on and on until the top of the 22nd inning. Then Jack Reed, a journeyman outfielder on the Yankees, who raised cotton in Mississippi during the off-season, cracked a home run to break it up.

The big Catfish that got away.

Charles O. Finley was the owner of the Oakland A's in 1975, when he let the big one get away.

Catfish Hunter had a contract that called for a salary of $100,000 a year with half of it—$50,000—to be paid directly to an insurance company for Hunter's family savings.

Finley forgot to pay, and Hunter's lawyer said the contract was not worth the paper it was written on. After examination of all the legal mumbo-jumbo, Hunter was ruled a free agent.

Because of Finley's blunder, he lost a great pitcher without getting a dime for him.

Hunter was able to get 3.75 million dollars from the Yankees for signing, proving that one man's blunder is another man's bonanza.

It was a good thing it didn't go 10.

Zack Taylor was the manager of the last-place Browns of 1949. In the final game of the season, in an attempt to entertain the fans, and to find out if he had any real pitchers that he may have overlooked, Taylor used nine different pitchers in nine different innings.

He found out what he already knew: the Browns had a bad pitching staff. Chicago's one pitcher, Billy Pierce, beat the Browns single-handed.

Eyesight of umpires tested.

To quote a few old lines:

> Breathes there a fan with soul so dead,
> Who never to the ump hath said,
> "Yer blind, you bum!"

The answer is undoubtedly no. It's the accepted belief of the baseball fan that no umpire can even see the mask in front of his face.

But back in 1911, National League prexy Thomas Lynch, himself a former umpire, finally became fed up with these never-ending slurs. Accordingly, he appointed a committee of oculists to test the vision of every arbiter in the league. The report showed that every umpire had 20/20 vision or better—indeed, in most cases their visual acuity was far above average.

Has this scientific evidence silenced the critics? Yes—except for two words: "Oh, yeah?"

The man who was forgotten in all the noise.

On October 3, 1951, Bobby Thomson hit "the home run heard round the world,"—the dramatic game-winner against the Dodgers that won the National League pennant for New York.

What may or may not have changed the course of that game and baseball history was this: Don Mueller slid into third base on Whitey Lockman's double, and fractured his ankle. He had to be carried off the field.

Clint Hartung, the Hondo Hurricane—he was from Hondo, Texas—came in to run for Mueller.

While all this was going on, Ralph Branca was warming up. Maybe he warmed up too much or maybe too little. Anyway, while Mueller was being forgotten in the clubhouse except by a doctor, Thomson won the pennant with a home run.

Population pennant.

In 1962, at the conclusion of the New York Mets' first spring-training camp, Casey Stengel called in the press and announced his starting outfield—Frank Thomas in left, Richie Ashburn in center, and Gus Bell in right. One reporter pointed out that Thomas had six children, Ashburn six, and Bell eight.

"Well," Stengel responded, "if they produce as well on the field as they do off the field, we'll win the pennant."

Bye-bye, Bobo.

Bobo Holloman, a husky righthanded pitcher, started his first Major League game against the Philadelphia Athletics on May 6, 1953.

He pitched a no-hit, no-run game in his first big league start, knocking off the A's, 6-0.

No other pitcher in baseball ever began his career in a more auspicious way.

Going, going, gone! That was the rest of Holloman's career. He won exactly two more games that season for the Browns, was dispatched back to the minors by year's end, and never surfaced again in the biggies.

"You never saw so many line drives caught in one game as we saw that day," said Bill Veeck, the St. Louis owner.

He could have been Johnny Unitas.

Jake Gibbs was a fine quarterback for the University of Mississippi. He was also a fine baseball player. He chose baseball over football as a career and batted .233 as a Yankee utility catcher.

He probably would have done better as a National Football League quarterback, but nobody will ever know.

It might have been a blunder for him to choose baseball over football, when football was his better sport, but there was one other consideration.

The Yankees gave Gibbs $100,000 to sign. That helped him make up his mind.

Jack of all trades.

On the final day of the 1967 season, Bert Campaneris of the Kansas City A's became a one-man team. He started the game at his regular position of shortstop, and then worked his way around the infield, then the outfield, and on to pitcher and catcher as the game progressed.

Nine innings, nine positions, all of them played well, a one-man team.

Somebody asked Campaneris what he did between innings. "I sell popcorn," he said.

Shoulda had Spooner sooner.

On September 22, 1954, the Brooklyn Dodgers started a lefthanded rookie pitcher by the name of Karl Spooner. He struck out 15 men in his first start, and shutout the Boston Braves.

But he soon came down with a sore arm, and was never a big winner. The cry in Brooklyn, as the Dodgers lost the pennant to the Giants was, "We shoulda had Spooner sooner."

Close, but no cigar.

The best losing effort in a World Series game was turned in by Bill Bevens of the Yankees on October 3, 1947, at Ebbets Field in Brooklyn.

That day, Bevens was wild but wonderful. He walked ten Dodgers, but he hadn't allowed a hit through 8⅔ innings. In the bottom of the 9th, there were two runners on with walks, when Cookie Lavagetto came up to bat for Eddie Stanky.

Bevens threw a high curve to Lavagetto for a ball. The next pitch was a high outside fastball, and Lavagetto cracked it on a line over the head of Tommy Henrich in right field and off the right field wall.

The runners—Al Gionfriddo and Eddie Miksis—raced for home as the ball bounced away from Henrich.

When Miksis slid home with the winning run on Lavagetto's double, Bevens couldn't stand it. He turned away, and a tear came to his eye, and a lump to his throat.

It was the best losing World Series game ever. No pitcher wants to break that mark.

Kill the Umpire!

Life was never tougher for umpires than it was in the 1880s and 1890s. "Kill the umpire" was no idle threat. In fact, several minor league umps lost their lives on the diamond, and numerous major league arbiters were assaulted by mobs. The umpire, of course, was a quite common target for pop bottles.

In the popular image of the day, the man in blue merited every bit of abuse that could be heaped upon him. Witness this little ditty, published in 1886:

Mother, may I slug the umpire,
  May I slug him right away?
So he cannot be here, mother,
  When the clubs begin to play?

Let me clasp his throat, dear mother,
  In a dear, delightful grip
With one hand, and with the other
  Bat him several in the lip.

Let me climb his frame, dear mother,
  While the happy people shout;
I'll not kill him, dearest mother,
  I will only knock him out.

Let me mop the ground up, mother,
  With his person, dearest, do;
If the ground can stand it, mother,
  I don't see why you can't too.

And boo to you, Bill Klem!

In 1913, the Pirates and the Giants were locked in a decisive series. Calling them behind the plate was Bill Klem, an umpire who demanded—and commanded—plenty of respect. It was a close contest. Nerves were on edge. The Pirates were giving tough old Bill Klem as much guff as they dared.

Klem was slowly building to a blowup. Toward the end of the game he erupted, and stalked over to the Pirate dugout. "Listen, you guys," he exploded, "I've taken just about enough. Any more razzing from you and I clear the bench. Get it?"

By their stricken silence, the Pittsburgh players indicated that they got it, all right. Klem strode back to the plate and readjusted his mask and chest protector. Next man to step into the batter's box was a rookie, sent in by manager Fred Clarke as a pinch hitter. The kid was so nervous that when he mumbled his name to Klem, Bill didn't hear it.

"C'mon now," barked Klem, "don't delay the game. Give me your name and be quick about it!"

The youngster swallowed fearfully and opened his mouth. "Boo!" he said hoarsely.

Klem blew his top. "That does it," he yelled. "You're out of the game. Get off the field!"

The abashed rookie retired to the bench in confusion. After a whispered consultation, Fred Clarke dashed onto the field to explain to the glowering Klem that the youngster, brand-new to the majors, had meant no offense. His name was Everett Booe!

Has anyone seen home plate?

On August 28, 1909, home plate was in its usual spot. But Bill "Dolly" Gray, Washington's pitcher, couldn't seem to find it.

In the second inning of a game against the White Sox, Gray was as wild as a goose chase, yielding seven passes in a row. In that one frantic frame, bounteous Bill donated a total of eight free rides.

Why didn't the manager remove him? Chances are he didn't want to kill a world's record.

Say it Ain't So, Joe.

Joe Jackson earned the sobriquet "Shoeless Joe" because that's the way he played ball back home in the "hollers" of South Carolina. When the hillbilly came to the majors, he was still illiterate, but he had accustomed himself to wearing spikes on the field.

After a five-game trial with Connie Mack's A's in 1908 and another in 1909, Jackson was traded to Cleveland. The Naps, as they were called then, sent him to the minors for more polishing.

In 1911, Jackson finally got the chance to play every day. And what a rookie year he had! He fielded brilliantly and hit .408. In the nine years that followed, Shoeless Joe never hit below .300, and three times topped .370. His lifetime mark of .356 was bettered only by Ty Cobb and Rogers Hornsby.

Yet Shoeless Joe's name cannot be found on any plaque in the Hall of Fame. Though his playing credentials are certainly worthy of Cooperstown, Jackson was one of eight White Sox players who conspired with gamblers to throw the 1919 World Series.

On September 28, 1920, Jackson left the Cook County Courthouse after confessing to his role in that plot. As he walked down the steps, surrounded by photographers and newsmen, Jackson was accosted by a ragged little boy who pleaded, "Say it ain't so, Joe!"

But it was so, and Jackson went back to South Carolina in disgrace. He and the seven other "Black Sox" were banished from baseball for life.

Commercial assimulation.

Baseball club owners made a large portion of their annual profit from such ancillary sources of income as concessions, scorecards, and advertising space on the outfield fences. Capitalists clamored for the opportunity to publicize their wares before the ballpark audience, and many were clever enough to link their product with the hometown team.

For example, one ad taken out in Brooklyn's Ebbets Field read: "Zack Wheat caught 400 flies last season; Tanglefoot flypaper caught 10 million."

Pardon my blooper.

As great a ballplayer as Lou Gehrig was, he never seized the public's fancy in the way Babe Ruth did. While The Babe made hundreds of thousands of dollars from public appearances, exhibitions, and endorsements, Larrupin' Lou hardly made a cent. He simply lacked Ruth's charisma—but then again, didn't everyone?

On one of the few occasions that Gehrig picked up an endorsement, he fumbled it. Once, he was signed to go on radio to plug a breakfast cereal called Huskies.

"To what do you owe your strength and condition?" the announcer asked.

"Wheaties," Gehrig replied.

The mortified Gehrig refused to accept any money for the commercial, but the company insisted. Huskies had gained more publicity from Gehrig's boner than the cereal could ever have achieved if the commercial had gone smoothly.

Caught in the act.

The Baltimore Orioles of 1894-96 were the best team baseball had seen up to that time, and the craftiest. Wee Willie Keeler, Hughie Jennings, John McGraw, et. al., were not above a discreet violation of the rules—if such would win them a game. Perhaps the most famous of the Baltimore tricks is the one that backfired.

Prior to the start of a home game, Oriole outfielders would plant a few baseballs in strategic spots in the tall outfield grass. Balls hit up the alleys or down the lines which looked like sure extra-base hits were miraculously held to singles.

One day, however, an opposing batter drove a ball up the alley in left field. Two Balitmore men converged on the ball. The left fielder snatched up the ball he had hidden in the grass, whirled, and tossed it back into the infield, holding the batter at first base in spectacular style. Unknown to the left fielder, his partner in center field had been able to reach the batted ball, which he tossed back to the infield.

When the umpire saw two balls coming in to second base, he was not slow to act. He awarded the game to the visiting team by forfeit.

Trio of Bear Cubs, and fleeter than birds.

The most famous double-play combination of all time is undoubtedly Joe Tinker, Johnny Evers, and Frank Chance of the Chicago Cubs. This trio entered the Hall of Fame as a unit, though only Chance was a truly outstanding player. Indeed, their fame as a superior double-play combo is due principally to Franklin P. Adams' famous poem:

> These are the saddest of possible words—
> "Tinker to Evers to Chance."
> Trio of bear cubs, and fleeter than birds—
> "Tinker to Evers to Chance."
> Ruthlessly pricking our gonfalon bubble,
> Making a Giant hit into a double—
> Words that are weighty with nothing but trouble:
> "Tinker to Evers to Chance."

The fact of the matter is that in the four years from 1906 to 1909—the peak of their career—the vaunted trio completed only 54 twin killings—an average of less than 14 a year! Compare this to the 217 double plays completed by the Philadelphia A's in 1949 alone.

Double the trouble.

Eugene Moore, Tony Cuccinello, and Baxter Jordan of the Braves had a field day against the Cardinals on August 25, 1936. They each batted twice in the first inning, as the Braves were scoring 12 runs.

In the first inning of that fracas, Moore, Cuccinello, and Jordan each hit two doubles in two at bats.

A hero is born in a wink.

Johnny Leonard Roosevelt Martin—Pepper Martin to baseball fans—put on one of the most amazing performances of any man who ever played in a World Series. It was against the A's in 1931.

Martin became an instant hero as he led the Cardinals to a 4-3 Series win over the A's with a .500 batting average, which included 12 hits, four doubles, a homer, five runs scored, five RBIs, five stolen bases, and a half-dozen stretched hits and extra bases.

When the Series started, Martin was considered a good, if not great player. At the end of that week, October 10, 1931, Martin was probably the most famous man in America.

Nuxhall began a 16-year major league career before he was 16-years-old.

On June 10, 1944, Joe Nuxhall, a lefthanded pitcher out of Hamilton, Ohio, pitched for the hometown Cincinnati Reds. When Nuxhall walked onto Crosley Field that day, he was 15 years old and 316 days.

After the 1966 season, Nuxhall retired with 16 years in the big leagues.

Baseball's longest game ran 26 innings.

The longest game in baseball history was played May 1, 1920. Brooklyn and Boston went at it for 26 innings. The score was 1-1, and the game was finally called on account of darkness.

Brooklyn got a run in the fifth inning and Boston tied it in the sixth inning.

After that, it was a long line of zips on the scoreboard until sundown.

George Wright—the Star of the Cincinnati Reds of 1869.

The star of the Cincinnati Red Stockings of 1869 was shortstop George Wright. Receiving $1,400, he was the team's highest-salaried player, and his heroics attest that he was worth every penny of it.

In the 66 games that the Reds played on their 12,000-mile tour, Wright batted .518, scored 339 runs, and belted 59 home runs.

I got it, you got it, we all got it!

The Mets were playing the Cards at the Polo Gounds in 1962. A fly ball went up in short left field. Left fielder Frank Thomas, shortstop Elio Chacon, and center fielder Richie Ashburn all went for it.

Chacon was moving back waving his hands, Ashburn was moving over, and Thomas was moving in.

Chacon began yelling, "I got it," in Spanish. Ashburn, who knew some Spanish, quickly pulled out of the way. Thomas, who knew no Spanish, ran with his head down and crashed into Chacon. The ball was dropped, and the game was lost.

Old folks at home.

Diomedes Olivo was 45 years old when he pitched his first game in relief in the Major Leagues for the Pirates against the Braves. He lasted for three years, and was 48 years old when he was released by the Cardinals. Whereupon he immediately went back to Mexico, and began pitching south of the border.

Paul Richards used a shuffle system.

The manager of the Baltimore Orioles, Paul Richards, once used four left fielders in the same game. Each came to bat once, and each failed to get a hit.

It hardly mattered as everybody else on the Orioles, on that day of September 14, 1960, got a hit—and the Orioles beat Detroit, 11-10.

Bobbles, Bungles, and Boots.

The Chisox didn't look good in their game against the Tigers on May 6, 1903. In the course of nine innings, the Chicagoans made 12 errors to tie the record for fumbles.

The Detroiters didn't gloat. Two years before, on May 1, 1901, in a game between the same two teams, it had been the Tigers who first set the record by booting an even dozen chances.

And on May 6, 1903, as the Chicagoans were kicking 12 balls, the Tigers showed their sympathy by fouling up six plays on their own. That's 18 errors—the most by any two teams in one game!

Little big man.

Bill Veeck, the owner of the St. Louis Browns, has always had a flair for entertaining the fans. On a quiet doubleheader day in St. Louis in 1951, as the American League was celebrating its 50th birthday, he came up with a doozy.

Under cover of darkness, he had slipped a circus midget named Eddie Gaedel into town. Veeck was going to use him as a pinch hitter.

In the first inning, Frank Saucier was taken out of the game, and Eddie Gaedel, standing 3 feet 7 inches and weighing 65 pounds, marched up to the plate wearing a St. Louis Browns' uniform.

The pitcher, Bob Cain, and the catcher, Bob Swift, conferred on how to pitch to a dwarf.

"Pitch him low," ordered Swift.

Cain bent over, took his sign, stared at the ferocious little man at the plate, peeked at his catcher sprawled out on the ground, and fired away.

Gaedel, ordered not to move, stood still as the pitch came in for a ball. Then another, and another, and another. Now he was motioned to first base, removed for a pinch hitter, and marched off the field to a standing ovation.

Eddie Gaedel, 26 years old and 43 inches tall, became the smallest man ever to play in a Major League game.

You could look it up.

Frank Howard hits one of his monsters.

Whitey Ford was the best pitcher the Yankees ever had, a Hall of Famer, a man who would win most of the big ones in his brilliant career for the Bronx Bombers. He rarely gave up a home run, but there was one blow, a real beaut, that he remembers through the years.

"Nobody ever hit a ball that hard off me," said Ford, "or anybody else." The blow was struck that October day in Los Angeles by Frank Howard, the huge right fielder of the Dodgers. Howard weighed in at 260 pounds, stood 6 feet 7 inches, and was known as Hondo—same as the Hurricane of the same name. He was considered the strongest man in the game.

On this day, Ford was engaged in a brilliant pitching duel with Sandy Koufax of the Dodgers. The Dodgers led 3-0 in games, and were trying for a sweep against the Yankees with their lefthander from Brooklyn, Koufax, going against the lefthander from Queens, Ford. There were 55,912 fans in the Dodger Stadium.

In the bottom of the 5th inning, Big Frank came to bat. He took a pitch from Ford, and then swung hard at the next one. "I ducked," said Ford. "I though it was a line drive right at the mound, and I didn't want to get hit by anything coming at me that fast." The "line drive right at the mound" continued to rise at it cleared second base. Mickey Mantle, in center field, went back slowly as if he was about to catch the ball. Then he suddenly turned, and gave up. The ball continued to rise in a huge arc, gain in speed, and then came crashing into the second tier at Dodger Stadium, more than 450 feet from home plate.

"All I can say about that one," said Ford, "is that I am very glad it wasn't a line drive at me. I'd probably still be running back if it was."

Why was he called "The Man?"

A fan in Brooklyn's Ebbets Field gave Stan Musial the name after he hit three homers and two doubles in one game against the Dodgers, and knocked in seven runs.

"Whatta man! Whatta man!" exclaimed the fan as he left the park.

From that day on, Stan "The Man," was the man the fans in Brooklyn came to watch.

BASEBALL'S ZANIES

There was the time Casey Stengel doffed his cap to the cheers of the crowd and a bird flew out of his hair and circled the field while the crowd roared.

There was the time Cuccinello loped into third base standing up and was put out. He didn't attempt a slide, he explained to his manager, because he was afraid he might bust some cigars in his pocket.

There was the time one of the Washington Senators sent a screaming drive into the left field stands. The umpire had run over to the left field line to judge the ball, and just then there was a woman being carried from the pavilion. The arbiter asked Coach Altrock whether the woman had been hit. "No!" answered Nick, so all the fans could hear. "You called that one right and she passed out from shock."

There was the time that Art Shires responded to the boos from the bleachers by turning to the crowd and shouting, "Good! That's all right. Go ahead. I get excited, too, when I see a great ballplayer!"

But these stories must stand for what they are—isolated antics in the baseball saga. The zanies whose histories follow are noted for consistent lunacy. They wrote the funny sheets for years. Rube Waddell, Babe Herman, Dizzy Dean, Goofy Gomez, Jackie Brandt, and Casey Stengel—each played baseball and screwball. And it is hard to tell which role has endeared them the most.

Rube Waddell

"Come and see Rube fan 'em out!" That inscription in huge painted letters on walls and sidewalks, was familiar to fans around the turn of the century. They knew who the artist was. He was a man who believed in advertising—self-advertising! He was advertising a long, gawky, easy-going, lefthanded pitcher named George Edward Waddell.

And Waddell wasn't boasting, for fan 'em out, he did. Again and again and again!

There are many who hold that Rube was the game's greatest pitcher. Certainly he was one of its greatest personalities. He was front-page copy for years.

Came two o'clock of a day the great Rube was scheduled to pitch— no one would be much surprised if Waddell turned up missing. He might have decided to go fishing. He might have donned a drum-major's shako and gone to join a parade. Or he may have decided to chase the fire-engines to a blaze. Once after a frantic search, he was located under the stands, shooting marbles with a bunch of kids!

Great player though he was, few managers could put up with the Rube for long. He was fired from club after club. Either Rube went—or the manager's sanity. Only Connie Mack seemed to know how to handle this loony southpaw.

One afternoon in a crucial series, Waddell pitched and won the first game of a double-header. During the intermission, Mack promised the Rube a day off to go fishing—provided he won the second game. That bait was all Waddell needed. He mowed 'em down like sandlot kids and then he streaked out of the park for his fishing trip.

Rube found one kindred soul on the Athletics—his battery mate, Ossie Schreck. Ossie roomed with him and became the partner in most of Waddell's escapades. Once Rube and Ossie stepped out for a big evening on the town. After hitting all the high sports, the two ballplayers drifted back to their hotel. Deciding that the evening was still young, they gathered their teammates to continue the celebration in their room.

Next morning Rube awoke aching all over—in a hospital room. He was encased in rolls of bandages. Painfully turning his head, the Rube saw his pal, Ossie, anxiously hovering over the bed.

"Oh-h," groaned the battered hurler. "How'd I get here? Last I remember, we was up in our rooms having a few drinks with the boys. What happened?"

"Don'cha remember?" said Ossie. "Long about midnight you suddenly got the idea you could fly. A couple of the boys said you wuz nuts, so you got mad and said you'd show 'em. Next thing I knew, you had the window open and out you hopped flappin' your arms, just like a bird."

"Holy cow!" howled the Rube. "I coulda been killed. Why didn'cha stop me?"

"What!" exclaimed Ossie in a tone of righteous indignation. "And lose the hundred bucks I bet you could do it?"

One day, Rube stormed into Connie Mack's office and announced that he was not going to sign his next contract. Since Waddell was the team's mainstay, Mack was prepared to make some concessions. "What's up, Rube?" he asked. "You want more money?"

"Naw, the dough's O.K.," Waddell admitted. "But I don't sign no more contracts unless it says in there someplace that that roommate of mine don't eat no more crackers in bed."

To save money, the club often arranged for Waddell and Schreck to sleep in the same bed. Ossie Schreck had a habit of munching soda crackers before going to sleep. Mack saw it Rube's way and Schreck's contract prohibited him from eating in bed.

George Edward Waddell's major league career was all too short because he never could beat old John Barleycorn. But at his best, few pitchers if any, could offer anything to compare with his magic. He was undoubtedly one of the best the game has ever known.

Babe Herman

Floyd Caves Herman was probably one of the most delightful characters on the American scene in the early 1930s. The lefthanded slugger of the Brooklyn Dodgers entertained more people than Al Jolson.

Like the great singer, every time Herman got into a ball park, fans were keyed up. They knew "they ain't seen nuthin' yet."

Herman's specialty was catching fly balls off his noggin.

Years later, Herman denied he had ever caught a fly ball off his head. Or not caught one, for that matter.

"Off the shoulders, yes," he protested, "but not off the head."

Herman was also less than a responsible base runner. His most famous play occurred in Brooklyn, in his rookie year of 1926.

The bases were loaded when Herman came to bat and smashed a long drive off the right field wall in Brooklyn. It looked like two runs for sure—maybe three—with Herman standing on third base with a triple.

Yet all the Dodgers got out of that great smash was one measly run. It happened this way. The man on third scored from third as the ball hit the wall. The man on second, watching the flight of the ball, raced to third and then stopped short figuring a strong throw might get him. The man on first, raced past second, and headed for third, just as the runner in front of him came back to third.

And now like a runaway locomotive, here comes Hoiman—as the fans in Brooklyn called him. He raced around first and second, and galloped towards third.

The first runner slid back into third. The second runner slid into third. And the last runner, the incredible Mr. Herman, also slid into third. Three runners on the same base! The third baseman tagged everybody in sight, including the umpire and the third base coach.

One man was called safe, two men were called out, and Hoiman was called a classic.

Herman once complained about his zanie image to a Brooklyn sportswriter.

"I'm a family man," he said. "my kids don't like reading that I'm a clown."

The sportswriter apologized and Herman said he would forgive him if he stopped writing that stuff. Then Herman reached into his pocket and pulled out a cigar.

"Here, I'll give you a light," said the sportswriter, in a spirit of friendship.

"Don't bother," said Herman, puffing a cloud of smoke, "it's already lit."

Dizzy Dean

Baseball rarely saw the likes of Dizzy Dean in more than 100 years of play.

Jay Hanna Dean joined the St. Louis Cardinals in 1930, won 18 games in 1932, and then came through seasons with 20 wins, 30 wins, 28 wins, and 24 wins. The following season he hurt his foot when hit by a line drive in the All Star game, and was forced to change his motion. Dizzy was out of baseball in 1941, even though he did make a guest appearance in 1947 with the Cardinals.

He was called Dizzy because he was a strange fellow, quick to laugh, and quicker to say something wild. Reporters even laughed when he gave them his name.

"I used to tell some of them my real name was Jay Hanna, and I used to tell others my real name was Jerome Herman," he said. "They all had to have a different story, didn't they?"

By any other name, he was a hard throwing righthander who teamed with his brother Paul, called Daffy.

One day, Dizzy pitched a two-hitter in the first game of a double-header against the Dodgers. Then Paul came to the mound, pitched a no-hitter against Brooklyn in the second game.

After the game ended, Dizzy marched up to his brother. Instead of congratulating Daffy, Dizzy was upset. "If I'da knowed you was goin' to pitch a no- hitter," said Dizzy, "I woulda done it, too." And he might have, too, because Dizzy was capable of doing almost anything on the mound.

At the beginning of the 1934 season, sportswriters asked Dizzy just what kind of a year he and Paul were about to have.

"Me and Paul, we're gonna win 45 games for the Cardinals and win the pennant," Dizzy said.

It sounded like terrible bragging. But it worked out even better than Dizzy said. Paul won 19 games, while ole Diz came up with 30 wins and the Cardinals won the pennant and the World Series.

After the 1937 season, Dizzy began going downhill as a pitcher, but never went downhill as a personality. He got into sports broadcasting, one of the first ball players to make that transition, and he revolutionized radio.

One day, the school teachers in Missouri made a formal complaint to the radio station Dizzy worked for. They said his poor grammar was influencing their students. Diz would say that the players were now going back to "their respectable positions," or he would tell how the pitcher "thowed" the ball, or he would call the man behind the plate the "empire."

What riled the teachers most was Dean's usage of "ain't." When the station manager told Dizzy about this, he replied with a smile, "Why shore I say *ain't,* but a lot of people who ain't saying *ain't,* ain't eatin'!"

Lefty Gomez

They called him Goofy, El Senor, the Gay Castillian, and a lot of other names in his pitching career—but nobody ever called him dull.

Vernon Louis Gomez came out of Rodeo, California to establish himself as one of the best lefthanded pitchers in the game with two 20-game seasons for the Yankees, and a winning percentage of .649 in his Major League career.

But Lefty Gomez is more famous for his antics than for his great pitching.

He was pitching in the World Series against the Giants when a plane flew overhead. Lefty had nothing better to do, so he studied the craft as it made a slow pass over the top of the roof at the Polo Grounds.

"Why, you screwball!" yelled manager Joe McCarthy, a conservative type, as the inning ended. "Keep your eye on the game, not the plane. I'm surprised they didn't start knocking the ball out of the park."

"How could they?" Gomez asked his manager with much logic. "All the time I was looking at the plane, I was holding on to the ball."

Gomez also was famous for bombarding his teammates with water bags from the height of his hotel window.

"Once, I was dropping some water bombs on my young teammate, Phil Rizzuto, when a nice lady walked by underneath and was splattered. I didn't go out of my room for the rest of the day for fear somebody would tell," he said.

Gomez used to have some fine pitching battles with Bobby Feller of the Indians. Feller really scared hitters with that blazer of his.

One day, on a gray afternoon, Gomez came to bat against Feller. He paused at home plate, took a match from his pocket and lit it up.

"Cut the comedy;" yelled the ump, "you think that will help you see Feller's fast one?"

"Shucks," said Goofy, "that's not what I'm worried about. I want to make sure Feller sees me."

Jimmy Piersall

From 1950 through 1967, Jimmy Piersall was an outfielder of almost unequalled skills. He was also a strong hitter, a fine base runner, and a marvelous entertainer. His antics, some intentional, some uncontrollable, entertained fans across the league.

In his book, "Fear Strikes Out," Piersall explained the pressures on him which actually led to a nervous breakdown and hospitalization. He spent too much time being what people wanted him to be, instead of being himself.

Piersall was so high-strung, and so emotional, it was impossible to figure when he would go off the deep end.

One time, he was playing centerfield in Yankee Stadium. The fans has a bad habit of jumping the small fence at the right field stands, coming on the field and shaking hands and asking for autographs of players while the game was in progress.

But when they picked on Piersall, they picked on the wrong guy.

Two spectators stormed out to centerfield. As soon as they got near Piersall, he yelled at them, scared them, and gave chase. He kicked one of them in the seat of his pants, guaranteeing that that fan wouldn't sit for the rest of the game.

Piersall played for the Boston Red Sox from 1950 through 1958. Then he drifted to Cleveland, Washington, the Mets, and the Angels.

One of his best days came with the Mets when he belted career homer number 100. To celebrate the event, Piersall turned around and began circling the bases backwards looking and laughing at the first baseman as he neared second, doing the same with the second baseman as he neared third, and to the third baseman as he neared home, and then to the catcher after he had crossed the plate.

Stengel was the manager of the Mets when Piersall went into his act. Casey didn't like it one bit.

"I'm the only clown around here," said Stengel, and he immediately fired Piersall.

Jackie Brandt

Jackie Brandt was a colorful outfielder with several clubs in the late 1950s and 1960s. During his time with Baltimore, from 1960-1965, he acquired the reputation of being a flake. In baseballese, a flake is an eccentric, a strange person, a weirdo with strange habits.

Consider this. Brandt was known by his teammates as being very fond of ice cream. One day, a teammate came up to him in spring training and informed him that a marvelous new ice cream parlor had opened some 25 miles away from the Baltimore training camp. It listed 44 flavors.

"Knowing how much you like ice cream," said the teammate, "I sure wish it was nearby."

"It's only 25 miles away," said Brandt, "let's go."

Three or four players piled into the car, and Brandt began whizzing down the highway to the fabulous new ice cream store.

"What'll you have?" asked the ice cream man as Brandt stood at the counter.

"Vanilla," he said.

PETE ROSE SIGNS FOR 3.2 MILLION DOLLARS

The highest paid baseball player ever.

On Tuesday, December 5, the baseball world was shocked when Pete Rose, who had become a free agent, signed a mind-blowing contract for 3.2 million dollars with the Phillies, the agreement covering four seasons.

The former third baseman of the Cincinnati Reds would be paid $800,000 a year for each of the next four seasons—ten times what Babe Ruth had been paid by the New York Yankees in 1927.

The 37-year-old player, known as Charley Hustle for his aggressive style of play, electrified baseball in 1978 with a hitting streak in 44 consecutive games, breaking the old National League record of 37 held by Tommy Holmes of Boston, and falling a dozen games short of Joe DiMaggio's famous 56-game consecutive hitting streak of 1941.

Rose also passed the 3,000-hit mark in 1978 becoming the 13th player to collect more than 3,000 hits. Going into the 1979 season, Rose had 3,164 hits, closing in on Stan Musial's record of 3,630 hits.

Peter Edward Rose, born April 14, 1941, joined the Cincinnati Reds in 1963 as a second baseman. He played second, third, and the outfield for the Reds, and is ticketed for first base with the Phillies. He has batted over .300 during 13 separate seasons, has won three batting titles, has collected over 200 hits in nine seasons, has starred in eight All-Star games and four World Series.

He will be the most closely watched player in 1979. If anybody is worth $800,000 a year for playing baseball, it is Pete Rose.

BIG MOMENTS
OF THE BIG TIME

Matty pitches his third shutout in 1905 Series.

Polo Grounds, New York, October 14, 1905

The awed crowd has come to see the magnificent Matty. He had blanked the A's on Monday with four hits and had repeated the performance on Thursday. Could he do it again?

After their first whitewash, Philadelphia had bounced back on Tuesday with Chief Bender to shellac the Giants with a shutout of their own. But in the third game on Thursday, Matty had beaten the A's again.

Now it was Saturday, and the score stood 3-1, in favor of the Giants. Could Matty drive the final nail into the Philadelphia coffin?

In the fifth inning, Chief Bender momentarily weakened. The Giants scored a solitary run. That was all Big Six needed. For the great Mathewson was well-nigh invincible as he held the enemy in check with six scattered hits.

When the last of the Athletics died swinging on that historic afternoon, the fans let out an enormous yell, for each and every one knew he had witnessed the making of an immortal record.

Merkle neglects to touch second base.

Polo Grounds, New York, September 23, 1908

One of the smartest, heads-up ballplayers ever to wear a major league uniform is remembered today by his wholly undeserved nickname of Bonehead Merkle. The nickname stemmed from one freak play, and he was never able to live it down. Here's the story.

The Giants, Pirates, and Cubs were bunched in a thrilling three-way race for the league lead in the closing weeks of the 1908 season. The Giants were at home playing a crucial series against the Cubs. In his first full game of the season for the Giants, Merkle was performing very creditably at first base.

Coming down the last half of the ninth, the game, an air-tight thriller, was tied up at 1-1. With two down, McCormick was on third and Merkle on first. Al Bridwell, Giant shortstop, was at bat. Bridwell came through, cracking a line drive into center field. It was a clean single, and McCormick romped home with the winning run. Merkle, running between first and second, saw his teammate cross the plate. Fred abruptly left the base paths and ran toward the dugout. He wanted to avoid the mob of jubilant New York fans who were already swarming out onto the field. There was nothing unusual about Merkle's act: the rookie was only doing what he had seen dozens of veteran big-leaguers do before him.

But amid the after-game confusion on the field, Johnny Evers, quick-thinking Cub second baseman, stood on the keystone, screaming at his teammates to throw him the ball. When umpire Hank O'Day trotted over to find out what all the rumpus was about, Evers insisted on his calling Merkle out on a force play. He claimed that Bridwell had to get to first to qualify the hit, and if Bridwell must occupy first, then Merkle was forced to second. If, argued Evers, Merkle was out on the play, then of course McCormick could not have legitimately scored. There was much to-do for a long while, but finally O'Day had to yield to Evers' unimpeachable logic.

By this time, the crowd was at flood tide on the field. There could be no question about resuming the game. With the score knotted at 1-1, the game was called. When the season finished two weeks later, the Cubs and Giants were still tied for first place. In the single game play-off, the Cubs triumphed 4-2, winning the pennant.

Giant fans never recovered from their disappointment and thereafter hung the monicker of Bonehead on a ballplayer who turned in 15 years of first-rate baseball.

Johnson wins a Series game after 17 years.

Griffith Stadium, Washington, October 10, 1924

"Washington, first in war, first in peace—and last in the American League." That was the popular quip about the Senators in the first decade of the century.

Even when Walter Johnson scaled the heights of pitching glory, the great speedball artist couldn't change his team's losing habits. It began to look as though the greatest hurler of them all might never get a chance to pitch in a World Series.

Fortunately, Johnson was durable as well as artful. In 1924, the great righthander still had enough stuff to win 23 and lose only 7. Seventeen years after he had started his major league career, Walter Johnson led the league in pitching. By now, the Senators had amassed enough batting power to crash through to their first pennant.

To Johnson went the honor of pitching the opener against the Giants. It was an extra-inning heartbreaker. The Giants won in the twelfth, 4-3.

In the fourth game, Johnson lost again. But Zachary and Mogridge won three games to keep the Senators in the race.

In the seventh and deciding game, with the count at three games apiece, Bucky Harris put relief pitcher Johnson in once again to face Bentley.

It was a lulu of a battle. When the ninth inning ended, the score was knotted at three runs apiece. Neither team scored in the tenth. Neither team scored in the eleventh. In the last of the twelfth with one out, Muddy Ruel, Washington backstop, caught one on the handle of his bat and popped a puny foul. Hank Gowdy, the Giant catcher, whipped off his mask and started after it. But here fate took a hand. Gowdy didn't notice that his mask had rolled in front of him. His eyes turned skyward, he jammed a foot plunk into the mask.

That was the break. Ruel made good his reprieve and lashed out a two-bagger. Johnson reached first on an error. Then Earl McNeely drove a hard grounder down to Freddy Lindstrom at third. It looked like a double-play, but the ball struck a pebble a yard in front of Lindstrom and it bounded over the third baseman's head into left field. Ruel crossed the plate with the winning run.

No one begrudged Johnson his victory. Even Jack Bentley was cheerful about it. "I guess the good Lord couldn't stand seeing Walter Johnson lose again," he said. So on two flukes in the twelfth inning, Walter Johnson fulfilled his lifelong dream of winning a World Series game!

The Babe hits three homers in a Series game.

Sportsman's Park, St. Louis, October 6, 1926

The great Babe was as helpless as an infant in the first three games of the 1926 World Series. The St. Louis mound staff had kept the Bambino well in check, allowing him only two measly hits in three games.

But in the fourth contest, the sleeping Babe awoke and started kicking with a vengeance. In the first frame, the Redbird twirler, Flint Rhem, had whiffed Earl Combs and Mark Koenig on seven pitched balls. When Ruth, number three in the Yankee batting-order, stepped to the plate the fans began to hoot, "Put in a pinch hitter!"

As his first offering, the confident Rhem served up a fast-breaking curve. Wham! By twisting his head quickly, Rhem could see a little white speck soaring high over the right field fence. The crowd was stunned into a silence so complete you could have heard a pin drop. But not the ball. That landed outside the park on Grand Avenue, some 400 feet from home plate.

There were two out again in the third frame when The Babe came up to bat. This time Rhem tried a slow floater. The change of pace didn't change his luck. The eyes of a startled crowd of Card rooters watched the pellet follow its predecessor in a non-stop flight over the right field stockade.

In the fourth, Reinhart, who had been rushed in as relief for the badly shattered Rhem, handled Ruth with more respect. He was taking no chances. Four balls over the outside of the plate were better than one over the fence. So Ruth got a walk.

But the cautious Reinhart couldn't afford such luxury in the sixth. Then, when the bulk that was Babe appeared in the batter's box, there were two men on. A pass would only mean that Reinhart would have to face Gehrig with the bases full—a nauseous prospect for any pitcher. So Reinhart elected to pitch.

The count stood 3 and 2; the crowd waited tensely. Reinhart tried to uncoil a fast one over the inside corner. Somewhere in mid-flight, the horsehide collided with four pounds of seasoned ash and changed its direction of travel.

The ball took a nonstop to the center field seats, a mere 450 feet away—the mightiest wallop ever generated in the Missouri park. This was Babe's third homer of the day, and a World Series record.

This time, as The Babe ambled around the bases with his usual ponderous grace, the crowd, silent and resentful on his first two drives, climbed to its feet and cheered!

You just couldn't stay mad at The Babe.

BABE RUTH HITS THIRD HOMER IN WORLD SERIES GAME Sportsman's Park, St. Louis, October 6, 1926. The great Bambino has just made a world's record. Even the disappointed St. Louis fans could not help but cheer this most remarkable exhibition of slugging power.

RUTH CROSSES PLATE AFTER WALLOPING A HOMER Yankee Stadium, New York, April 12, 1932. Gehrig extends a congratulatory hand to Ruth, as The Babe tallies after a circuit-smash. The A's catcher stands by speechless.

Alexander fans Lazzeri in the World Series.

Yankee Stadium, New York, October 10, 1926

For sheer, concentrated diamond drama, little can match the seventh inning of the seventh game of the 1926 World Series. The Yankees, heavy favorites, were old hands at the classic. The underdog Cardinals, fresh from their first league pennant, were eagerly battling to crown the season with the world's championship. The amazing fact—that the Series went into the final game tied at three games apiece—was due, in no small degree, to the efforts of a used-up old Cardinal hurler named Grover Cleveland Alexander.

Ol' Pete, then 40 years old and a veteran of 16 years in the majors, was well past his prime. But he still had enough stamina to muffle the murderous Yankee bats and win the second game of the Series handily. In the sixth game, too, just the day before, Alex had gone the full nine-inning route to defeat the Yankees a second time, and even up the Series.

Now, in the seventh and decisive game, the Redbirds held on for dear life to a razor-thin 3-2 lead. The St. Louis hurler, Jess Haines, was working craftily and effectively despite a blister that was beginning to form on his middle finger. But in the seventh, Haines began to falter. He walked Earl Combs, the first Yankee to face him. On a sacrifice by Koenig, Combs moved to second, and The Babe came up. This was no time to trifle with the Bambino's ruthless bludgeon, so Jess handed him an intentional pass. Haines won another momentary reprieve when Meusel's grounder forced Ruth to second. Two down.

But now Jess' finger was giving him real trouble. Four wide ones put Lou Gehrig on first, and the bases were full. And at the bat pile, picking out his club was eager, hard-hitting, young Tony Lazzeri.

From second base, Manager Rogers Hornsby called time. He walked to the pitcher's box and inspected Haines' damaged digit. The blister had opened and was bleeding. The Rajah looked up and beckoned to the bullpen, where Flint Rhem and Art Reinhart were warming up. But the signal was not for either of them. A third man—a hunched, shambling figure—started toward the infield. Grover Cleveland Alexander shuffled in to keep a date with diamond destiny.

The suspense of the moment made that slow walk in from the bullpen seem interminable. From the hushed silence in the stands it might easily have been the death march.

Why, many wondered, was it Alexander, and not Reinhart or Rhem, coming in toward the mound? After his nine-inning chore of the day before, Ol' Pete had no reasonable expectation he would be called on again. In view of that he had done some celebrating—perhaps a little too much celebrating—the night before. Was he rested enough—was he in condition to pitch?

Hornsby met him at the sideline. For a moment the manager looked into the old hurler's eyes. What he saw there reassured him. Hornsby said quietly, "Go to it. You can do it, Pete."

Alexander's first toss was a feeler. Lazzeri refused to bite. Ball one. Then came a low fast one. A called strike. One and one. Tony lashed at the next one.

The piercing crack was like a rifle report. Sixty thousand fans jumped to their feet howling, as a mighty line drive whistled toward the left field stands. The ball zoomed over the fence and the shouts rose to a deafening roar—and then suddenly died away. The drive was foul by a foot! The disappointed Yankee runners retreated to their bases.

Alex wound up again. Everything the aging arm had left went into the next pitch. Lazzeri took aim, swung venomously—and missed! Strike three!

For all practical purposes, that ended the ball game. Alex set down the Yanks without much trouble in the eighth and ninth frames, and Herb Pennock of the New Yorkers returned the compliment. The 3-2 score stood, and the hysterical Cards carried the Series crown back to St. Louis.

LAZZERI STRIKES OUT WITH BASES FULL.

Old man Ehmke wins the World Series opener.

Wrigley Field, Chicago, October 8, 1929

The crowd could scarcely believe their ears when the starting battery for the Athletics was announced. In the Philadelphia dugout the players stared at each other in dismay. Across the field, on the Cubs' bench, the jubilation was unrestrained. Old Howard Ehmke going to start the Series opener? Someone must be crazy—and that someone could only be Connie Mack!

It was true that Ehmke had once been a stellar moundsman, but everybody knew he was through. That season he had pitched only two complete games for the A's. When the club took its final western swing, Ehmke hadn't even been taken along. Everybody knew Ehmke was a has-been—but here he was going to start the all-important first game of the Series!

Connie Mack had ordered Howard Ehmke to stay home to rest his arm. The wily pilot had sent him to scout the Cubs who had already clinched the National League flag. If Ehmke felt the the old soupbone could go the route, Mack had promised to start him. Maybe it was a sentimental promise. But Mack was as good as his word.

Few would have been surprised to see the old-timer blasted out of the box in the first inning. But as the afternoon wore on, Ehmke proved that his old craft was still there. His long rest and the welcome rays of the warm October sun combined to loosen up and restore zip to the old muscles. Yes, Ehmke was in there pitching!

Inning after inning, the baffled Cubs went down before the old master's sleight-of-hand. They got hits, yes—eight of them. But they couldn't bunch them to push across a run. In the pinch, old Howard still had what it takes. He fanned the great Rogers Hornsby twice. Slugging champ Hack Wilson also took the three-strike treatment on two trips to the plate.

Going into the ninth, Ehmke had fanned 12 men, tying the World Series record set in 1906 by Big Ed Walsh. The Cubs had yet to score.

But in the ninth, it began to look as though the old firehorse had shot his bolt. With the A's guarding a 3-0 lead, the Cubs began to reach Ehmke. The rescue squad began to warm up in the A's bullpen. The Cubs had shoved a run across the plate. With two out and two tying runs on base, a Cub pinch hitter came to bat.

Could old Howard bear down just once more? Did Ehmke have

enough reserve to come through in the vital pinch? The washed-out vet summoned all the experience of his years—summoned the last ounce of energy left in his quivering frame.

In spite of themselves, the Chicago fans couldn't help cheering as the pinch hitter went down swinging for the 13th strikeout of the game—a World Series record at that time.

Connie Mack had gambled on getting one more good game out of the fading Howard Ehmke, and a great pitcher hurled an immortal game.

HOWARD EHMKE WINS WORLD SERIES OPENER Ehmke pitching for the Athletics against the Chicago Cubs in first World Series game. He stayed for nine innings and set record of 13 strikeouts, amazing the baseball world.

A's 10-run rally overcomes Cub's 8-run lead.

Shibe Park, Philadelphia, October 12, 1929

The score was so one-sided it was practically no contest. A few prudent fans left the park early to miss the rush. The prudent missed the most astounding rally in World Series history.

Coming up to the last half of the seventh, it looked as though the Cubs had the game iced away in a deep freeze. They were atop an 8-0 score. Their pitching ace, Charlie Root, had been practically inaccessible.

Came the seventh, the first man up for the A's, Al Simmons, poled out a home run. That didn't worry the Cubs much. After all, it was only one run.

But then a staccato of singles rattled off the bats of Jimmy Foxx, Bing Miller, Jimmy Dykes, and Joe Boley. Two more runs crossed the plate, and the mastodonic lead of eight was whittled down to a mere colossal five.

When pinch hitter George Burns popped to the infield, it looked as if Charlie Root was once more in control. But Max Bishop promptly singled, driving still another run across. This was enough for Manager Joe McCarthy, and he sent an SOS to the Cub bullpen. The veteran Art Nehf, came in to replace Root. With the score 8-4, the brooding Philly crowd was beginning to come to life, though to the unprejudiced, the four-run lead seemed as solid as the south.

Mule Haas brought the fans to their feet with a whistling line drive to deep center. And then came the big break. Hack Wilson lost the ball in the glaring sun. Before he recovered the ball, Haas had rounded all bags, following two runs ahead of him. That made the score 8-7, but at least the bases were now clear.

They didn't stay that way long. The shaken Nehf passed Mickey Cochrane. That washed him up. McCarthy sent in Sheriff Blake to stem the tide.

Now Al Simmons came to bat for the second time. He celebrated this fact with a solid single. Jimmy Foxx followed up with another smash that propelled Cochrane across with the tying run. Sheriff Black went off to write his memoirs.

When Pat Malone, the fourth Cub pitcher, took his place behind the rubber, there was Simmons perched on third and Foxx dancing off first. To keep the proceedings from getting into a rut, Malone hit Bing Miller with a pitched ball, thus filling the bases. And when Jimmy Dykes punched out a vicious double, scoring Simmons and Foxx, all pandemonium broke loose.

With no relief in sight, Malone struck out Boley and Burns to wind up the massacre. That ended the biggest inning in World Series history. Evidently, in baseball, a game isn't over—well, 'til it's over!

DYKES OF THE ATHLETICS STEALS HOME DURING A'S 10-RUN RALLY In third game of World Series, A's behind 8-0 made 10 runs. Gabby Harnett is behind plate for the Cubs.

THE ATHLETICS' MURDERERS ROW Here are the five big guns who jammed home 10 runs in one inning of historic World Series rally. These men boasted a batting average of over .341 for the 1929 season. From left to right, Bing Miller, Mickey Cochrane, George Haas, Al Simmons, Jimmy Foxx.

Babe Ruth calls his shot.

Wrigley Field, Chicago, October 1, 1932

No one but The Babe would have been brash enough to try it. No one but The Babe would have gotten away with it. Set against the magnificent backdrop of the 1932 World Series, it provided one of the most dramatic climaxes ever recorded in baseball.

It was a grudge battle. The Cubs, floundering in mid-season, had bought shortstop Mark Koenig from the Yanks. Koenig outdid himself with Chicago, sparkling at bat and in the field as the Cubs went on to win the National League flag. When the World Series shares were revealed, however, it was found that Koenig had been shortchanged, awarded only a one-half share of the spoils. That caused The Babe to label the Cubs as "cheapskates."

The Chicago fans had been riding The Babe unmercifully. On the field, the Cubs—stung by two defeats—were also taking it out on The Babe. The catcalls rose to a crescendo when the hulking, spindly legged Babe stepped to the plate in the top half of the fifth. The score stood knotted at 4-4. There was one out and the bases were empty.

Charlie Root split the plate with a sizzling beauty—a perfect strike. The Babe beat the ump to the gesture when he raised his right index finger in token of *Strike One!* The rabid crowd howled its glee.

Root wound up again and zipped another pitch down the groove. The Babe didn't wait for Umpire Van Graflen to call this one either. With a grin he raised two fingers in the air, calling *Strike Two!* on himself. From the stands, there issued an unholy roar of delight.

Ruth stepped out of the batter's box waiting for the hubbub to die down. The clatter only rose to new heights. In anticipation, the fans were tasting the joy of seeing the mighty Babe, the fabulous Sultan of Swat, strike out.

It was then that Ruth made his immortal gesture of defiance. He lifted his hand and pointed—pointed toward the flagpole in deep center field. "That," said the gesture, "is where the next pitch is going to go."

And that is exactly where the ball went! On Root's next pitch, The Babe swung from his ankles and sent the ball soaring far into the field. It landed but a few feet to the side of the flagpole into the center field bleachers!

Stunned, the Chicago fans sat speechless as the grinning Babe cruised triumphantly around the bases.

Hubbell strikes out
the Yankees powerhouse squad.

The Polo Grounds, New York, July 10, 1934

Lefty Gomez, the hard-throwing Yankee pitcher, was a big winner and a Hall of Fame pitcher. He also was one of the worst batters ever to play the game. He not only was a poor hitter, he was awkward, falling down, slipping over himself, making the art of hitting a ball look like something only a Houdini could accomplish.

Despite all this, if it weren't for his Hall of Fame teammate, Bill Dickey, Gomez would be listed with the greatest hitters in the 1934 All-Star game at the Polo Grounds.

King Carl Hubbell, the crafty lefthander of the Giants, was throwing his devastating screwball at the American League stars that day. It took Hubbell a little while to get going, as Charlie Gehringer started out for the American Leaguers with a single, went to second on an error by center fielder Wally Berger, and stayed there as Heinie Manush drew a walk. With two on and nobody out, Hubbell had the meat of the American League order staring into his bony face. In front of him were Babe Ruth, Lou Gehrig, Jimmy Foxx, Al Simmons, Joe Cronin, Bill Dickey, and Goofy Gomex.

Well, Hubbell wasn't all that afraid of Goofy Gomez, but those other big belters could scare a pitcher out of his shoes. Hubbell took a deep breath, and went to work. He started firing that screwball—a pitch that bends into a lefthanded hitter when thrown by a lefthander.

The Babe took one pitch, then took two mighty rips. Thank you, Babe. Next batter.

It was Lou Gehrig, a mean man with the lumber, a hitter who was very smart, and was rarely fooled. Hubbell didn't fool him, he just whiffed him with three of the nastiest breaking balls The Iron Horse had ever seen.

Now it was two out, two on, and Jimmy Foxx, a righthanded slugger at bat. Could King Carl pull his tricks on the righthanded star just as he had on the two lefties? He could, and he did as the home crowd of Giants fans went wild in the Polo Grounds. Three straight strikeouts on baseball's three greatest hitters.

Owen drops third strike.

Ebbets Field, Brooklyn, October 5, 1941

"I was a rookie shortstop that day," remembers Phil Rizzuto of the Yankees, "and my job was to collect the gloves before the final out, so the kids wouldn't rush on the field and take them. I was sitting there with the gloves on my lap when it happened. The next thing I know, I was spilling gloves here and there and everywhere."

The Yanks were playing the Dodgers in the 1941 World Series. Hugh Casey, the fine relief pitcher for Brooklyn, was on the mound. He had a 4-3 lead, and the Yanks had two out in the top of the ninth. One more batter and the Brooks would have a win in game four. The Series would be tied 2-2.

Brooklyn had never won a World Series, and this was their best chance. The last batter was Tommy Henrich, "Old Reliable" of the Yankees, a guy who got his nickname because he always seemed to do something important in the clutch.

Casey worked carefully on the Yankee right fielder and had two strikes on him when it happened. The husky Dodger relief pitcher—bending the rules ever so slightly—moistened the baseball a bit and threw a spitter at Henrich. The ball dipped and danced as it came to home plate. Henrich swung and missed the pitch by a foot and the game was over.

But wait. Whoops! Isn't that catcher Mickey Owen racing back to the backstop? Faster than a speeding bullet, he moved, as Henrich raced to first base. The game was over, but it wasn't because Owen had missed the third strike and Henrich was on first. He didn't stay there long, as Casey allowed a single to Joe DiMaggio, a double to Charlie Keller, a walk to Bill Dickey, and a double by Joe Gordon for four Yankee runs.

The Dodgers were as flat as a pancake in their half of the ninth, and in the next game as well, and the Series was over.

"Holy cow," exclaimed Rizzuto. "We lost it and we didn't."

MICKEY OWEN DROPS THIRD STRIKE Ball at the tip of Owen's mitt is rolling towards dugout. Henrich has just completed his swing. Owen races for ball as Henrich heads for first. Umpire Goetz is calling Henrich out on third strike.

Lavagetto breaks up Bevens' no-hitter.

Ebbets Field, Brooklyn, October 3, 1947

It was the fourth game of the World Series in the ninth inning, and all that stood between big Floyd Bevens and baseball immortality was one out. One single, solitary out—three strikes, or a captured fly, or a fielded grounder—any one of those would have given the lumbering Yankee righthander the first and only no-hit game in World Series history.

Bevens had plenty of stuff that afternoon, but he couldn't always control it. He had walked eight men. Two of these passes, blended with a sacrifice and a force play, had put a run across for the Dodgers. But going into the ninth, it was indisputably a no-hit game, and the Yanks were ahead by a score of 2-1.

With one out in the final stanza, Bevens still a mite shy of control, walked Carl Furillo. Then Spider Jorgenson flied out. Two down and only one to go!

Pete Reiser, still limping from an ankle injury suffered the day before, went in to pinch hit for the Dodger's relief hurler Hugh Casey. Bevens tried to get him to bite on some bad ones. No dice. The count went to three balls and no strikes. Now Bevens was faced with the unpleasant choice of grooving one for Pistol Peter or of handing him a free pass. He looked toward the bench for instructions.

Manager Bucky Harris of the Yankees elected to violate the old baseball adage, "Never walk the winning run to first." He signaled Bevens to walk Reiser.

Now it was Burt Shotton's turn to do some masterminding for the Brooklyn Dodgers. After sending in Eddie Miksis to run for the ailing Reiser, Shotton turned toward the bench. He jerked his thumb at Lavagetto.

A tremor of excitement passed through the Dodger dugout. Shotton was sending the once-able, but now fast-fading Cookie as a pinch hitter. And to take the place of Eddie Stanky, Brooklyn's reliable lead-off man! Doubt in the dugout was so thick you could slice it with a fungo bat.

Lavagetto stepped into the batter's box, and Bevens buckled grimly to his task. If he could only get over this last hurdle, World Series glory would be his. The bench-ridden Lavagetto pulled nervously at his belt.

Big Floyd wound up and scorched one straight down the slot. Lavagetto swung—and missed! Only two strikes to go! Now to tempt him to swing at a bad one. The big righthander prepared to waste one. He threw it high and outside. Lavagetto swung again—and connected.

Tommy Henrich in right field started running at the sound of ball meeting bat. He arrived at the concrete wall just a fraction of a second after the horsehide. Taking the ball on the first bound, Henrich flung it homeward. It reached the plate a bare second after the flying spikes of Eddie Miksis clicked across with the winning run.

Lavagetto had come through with the Dodgers' only hit of the afternoon. Though Cookie was the toast of a delirious Brooklyn, still many fans who were thrilled no end by the great pinch hit, were also mindful of the tragic disappointment of big Floyd Bevens who had come within two strikes of a World Series no-hitter and everlasting fame.

LAVAGETTO IS CONGRATULATED BY TEAMMATES Surrounded by back-thumping Dodger teammates, policemen, guards, and fans, Cookie Lavagetto has become the hero of Flatbush after pinch-hitting his historic double. Jackie Robinson, Ralph Branca, Al Gionfriddo, and Gene Hermanski are in the picture. No. 4 is Eddie Miksis.

Thomson's homer wins playoff.

Polo Grounds, New York, October 3, 1951

It is by far the most famous home run in baseball history, known as *The Home Run Heard Round the World.* Years later, people would ask friends, "Where were you the day Bobby Thomson hit it?" People would measure time by the moment the ball crashed into the left field seats.

The game was the third of the 1951 pennant playoff between the Brooklyn Dodgers and the New York Giants. These two old rivals had battled for years.

In 1951, the Dodgers had driven ahead to a 13½ game lead on August 11. There would be no joy in the Polo Grounds this year.

But wait! Suddenly the Giants were winning, and the Dodgers were losing. The lead began to dribble away, ten games, five games, two games, finally a tie, after the final game of the season.

A playoff would begin in Brooklyn. The Giants won the first game, the Dodgers won the second, and in the third, Brooklyn led 4-1 in the ninth. Alvin Dark and Don Mueller singled; Whitey Lockman doubled. The score was 4-2, and Don Newcombe, the big righthander of the Dodgers, was out of the game.

The pitcher for Brooklyn was Ralph Branca—who got the call over Carl Erskine, who was also warming up in the bullpen. "Erskine just bounced a curve," said bullpen coach Clyde Sukeforth, over the phone to manager Charley Dressen. It was as famous an expression in Brooklyn years later, as General Custer shouting at Little Big Horn, "Where did all those Indians come from?"

Now Branca was pitching 0-1 to Thomson, the Staten Island Scot. Thomson swung, and the ball raced for the wall. Andy Pafko backed up in left. Thomson watched the flight. "God, make it come down," whispered Branca as he studied the line drive. But it cleared the wall easily, and the Giants won the pennant, as their players went wild on the field, hugging and mobbing Thomson.

In baseball, with one man's joy there is always some other man's sorrow, Branca later sprawled on the steps of the Dodgers clubhouse at the Polo Ground muttering, "God, why me?"

DUROCHER RESTRAINED AS THOMSON TROTS HOME Crazy with joy, Giants' manager
Leo Durocher is restrained by back-riding Ed Stanky as Bobby Thomson (left) trots around
third after hitting ninth-inning three-run, pennant-winning homer. Stanky has run out from
the dugout to get Leo off the baseline as the runners dash by him on their way to score.

Podres wins crucial Series game.

Yankee Stadium, New York, October 4, 1955

"The Brooks are jinxed!" everybody was saying as the seventh and deciding game of the 1955 World Series got underway. Five times before, Dodger pennant-winners had met the high-flying Yankees in Series play—and five times Brooklyn had gone down to bitter defeat before the potent warclubs and the stellar pitching of the Bronx Bombers.

Even though the ever-faithful Dodger rooters still refused to give up, the experts were laying odds on the Yankees to wrap up the championship—especially since the final game was being played on the New Yorkers' home grounds.

When Dodger manager Walt Alston called on pitcher Johnny Podres to carry the lead on the crucial day of October 4th, the old-timers shook their heads in disbelief. Sure Johnny had won the third game of the series for the Brooks only a few days before. But now the Dodgers were in too tight a spot to depend on a 23-year-old kid.

Against young Podres, who had lost more games than he'd won during regular season, canny Yankee manager Casey Stengel sent his ace hurler, veteran Tommy Byrne. Casey had led the Bombers to five World Series triumphs, and he had every intention of making it six. He knew that steady Tommy would be ice-cold when it counted—but would Podres crack under the terrific pressure?

Podres got into trouble early in the game, when hard-hitting Yogi Berra led off the fourth inning by dropping a double into left center. But Berra died on base as Johnny bore down. When the Brooks got to Byrne for two hard-earned runs, Dodger rooters began to dream of the impossible—a World Series crown, the first in the long history of the valiant Ebbets Fielders.

But the Yankees hadn't given up yet! In the bottom half of the sixth, Yankee runners reached second and third with none out. The Bombers threatened to break the game wide-open. Plucky Podres, helped by a magnificent catch by little left fielder Sandy Amoros, pitched his way out of hot water.

In the eighth, New York's powerful bats spoke loudly again. With only one out, the tying Yankee runs were on first and third. Cool and collected, as if he had made a habit of mowing down fearsome Yankee sluggers all his life, Podres retired the side. Not a single, solitary run could be scored against Johnny. It was his day, and the greatest day in the annals of Dodgerdom. When the last Yankee had succumbed to Podres' masterful pitching in the ninth, a tremendous roar from more than 60,000 throats shook the vast confines of Yankee Stadium. The mighty Yankees had been beaten, shut out by young Podres in their own backyard!

After seven fruitless and heartbreaking attempts, the Dodgers finally had won a world's championship. No wonder there was dancing in the streets of Brooklyn! No wonder that Brooklyn fans went completely wild! And no wonder that Johnny Podres will never be forgotten for having given one of the greatest exhibitions of clutch pitching in the history of the game.

JOHNNY PODRES PITCHES IN DECISIVE WORLD SERIES GAME The 23-year-old Dodger southpaw shut out the New York Yankees, 2-0, in the last Series game, bringing Brooklyn its first world championship in eight attempts.

Larsen pitches no-hitter in World Series.

Yankee Stadium, New York, October 8, 1956

There is hardly any pressure in baseball equal to the pressure of a World Series game, all that prestige riding, all that money, the fans of both teams anxious for victory. The rivalry between the Dodgers and Yankees in the Series of 1956 had become sensational.

In 1955, with Johnny Podres winning two games, the Dodgers had finally won a World Series.

Now it was 1956, the fifth game of the Series, and Don Larsen, a tall, crew-cut righthander facing Sal (The Barber) Maglie at Yankee Stadium. Larsen had been belted around in his first start in the Series in game number two, and was so depressed he told friends he was thinking of quitting baseball. Instead of quitting, he went on to pitch a game as memorable as any ball game ever played.

Larsen had adopted a new style of pitching that year. He delivered to the batters without a windup. He would get the sign, rock, and throw, without lifting the baseball or his gloved hand over his head. It had worked well, and now he was continuing with it through the Series.

He hadn't done well in his first start, but had much better stuff in his second, as he raced through the Dodger lineup—Jim Gilliam, Pee Wee Reese, Duke Snider, Jackie Robinson, and the rest, going down before the blazing fastball and crackling curve of the Yankee fireballer for seven innings. In the eighth—three up, three down—for Brooklyn.

Now it was the ninth. Carl Furillo was out. Roy Campanella was out. Sal Maglie was the scheduled Brooklyn hitter. Dale Mitchell, a lefthanded pinch hitter, was sent in to bat for "The Barber." Larsen took a deep breath, and threw a ball. Then a strike! Then a fastball over the plate, and then a foul. One strike away, just one swing and Larsen would be a baseball immortal. But just one bad pitch, one bloop single, and he would be a bum. He stepped back from the plate, rubbed his crew cut, studied Mitchell, and fired.

The pitch was a tick off the plate, at the knees. Umpire Babe Pinelli of the National League studied it for a split second—it seemed an hour to Larsen—and finally threw up his right hand and boomed, "Strike three! Y'er outta there!"

Larsen had a no-hitter, a perfect game, 27 men up, 27 men down! The only time in World Series history.

LARSEN'S LAST PITCH FOR PERFECT GAME Yankee pitcher is one pitch away from perfect pitched game. He stands head bowed with back to batter thinking what to throw to pinch hitter Dale Mitchell of the Dodgers. He touches his fingers to the resin bag for a second, then straightens up and fires the third strike to become the first pitcher who ever hurled a perfect game in a Series.

Burdette wins his third game in the 1957 Series.

Yankee Stadium, New York, October 10, 1957

"Look Lew," said Manager Fred Haney after the Braves had lost the sixth game. "Spahn is down with the flu. He's too weak to pitch. I'm counting on you. I know you've only had two days rest, but you're the best I have."

Haney knew what he was talking about. Burdette had won the second game, 4-2 to tie the Series. Then he shut out the Yanks, 1-0 in the fifth contest to give Milwaukee a 3-2 edge. He had blanked the Bombers for 15 straight innings.

Many observers felt that Haney was stretching his luck. Burdette couldn't continue. The Yanks were sure-fire bets to take him apart.

Opposing Burdette was Don Larsen, who only the year before had become the first hurler to pitch a perfect Series game.

When Stengel announced before game time that the mighty Mickey Mantle who had been out with injuries would be back again in action in the final fracas, things looked serious for Burdette and the Braves.

And when Hank Bauer opened the first inning by hitting Burdette's first pitch for a double, things looked glum.

But right then and there, the big righthander settled down. He retired the next three batters in apple-pie order.

In the third frame, the Braves let loose with a four-run barrage that shelled Larsen from the box. Now Burdette had something to work on. But could he keep that lead?

The Yanks got another man on base when Jerry Coleman singled in the fifth. But Burdette held New York at bay and Lew's scoreless inning streak had now reached 20.

Then Del Crandall unloaded a homer in the eighth, making the score Milwaukee 5, New York 0.

Came the last half of the ninth. The 60,000 fans grew tense as the Bomber bats were arrayed for a last stand. The first Yank up was retired. Now Burdette and the gallant Milwaukee Braves needed only two more outs for them to win their first world championship.

But Gil McDougall singled; and although Tony Kubek was counted as the second out, Coleman outlegged an infield hit, and Tommy Byrne got another.

The bases were loaded! Burdette was tiring. The Yankee fans were agog as their big rally seemed to take shape. Yankee luck! Yankee pluck! Would it pull them through at the very last minute as it had so many times in the past? Would Burdette be jinxed by the fabulous Yankees?

All eyes turned to the long, lanky figure in the pitcher's box. Burdette delivered. Skowron connected, banging a sharp grounder down the third base line. It looked like a hit! But Ed Mathews, his back to the ball, scooped it up and stepped on third to end the game.

Burdette had completed one of the most outstanding exhibitions of sustained pitching mastery of all time. He had blanked the Yanks for 24 consecutive innings. He had given Milwaukee its first world championship.

LEW BURDETTE IN NINTH INNING OF DECISIVE WORLD SERIES GAME.

Sherry brings first title to Los Angeles.

Comiskey Park, Chicago, October 8, 1959

The scoreboard told the tale: "Dodgers 8, White Sox 0." The crowd of 48,000 fans assembled in Comiskey Park sat back, hushed, and just about resigned to a horrendous shellacking of their heroes.

It was the last of the fourth inning. Johnny Podres, Los Angeles southpaw, was mowing down the Sox batters.

One Sox batter had bitten the dust, when Landis got to first after being struck by a pitched ball. Then Sherm Lollar walked, putting Chicago runners on first and second. Up strode mighty Ted Kluszewski, a muscleman who had already belted out two homers in the Series. The spectators suddenly woke up. "Go, go, go," they shouted.

There was a sharp crack as "Big Klu" connected. The ball streaked like a meteor 400 feet up into the right field stands. The White Sox had narrowed the gap to 8-3.

Visibly shaken, pitcher Podres handed Al Smith a base on balls. Dodger manager Walter Alston took this as the warning signal to virtually leap from the dugout. He had a few words with Podres, then signaled the bullpen.

No one had to be told who the new pitcher was. Alston was going with his best. He *had* to. The Dodgers needed but a single victory to wrap up the first world championship for Los Angeles. And the player who had done quite a lot to prepare this prize package was now approaching the pitcher's mound. His name was Larry Sherry.

This was the unknown who had come up to L.A. from the minors late in June—the kid who had gone on to spark the Dodgers to a pennant.

Then came the Series. The Dodgers were up against a speedy, aggressive team with loads of talent. The "Go Go" Sox showed their sparkling class in the first game, blanking L.A. 11-0. In the second game, after the Dodgers took a 4-2 lead in the seventh, Manager Alston again entrusted Sherry with a chips-are-down chore. Again Larry came through, yielding only a single run in the final three innings.

With the Dodgers ahead 2-0 in the eighth inning of the third game, pitcher Drysdale lost his stuff. He had given up one run and the Sox had a couple of runners on the bases, when in strolled Fireman Sherry to douse the Sox rally under a deluge of curves and fastballs.

The following day Sherry was again a hero. With the score knotted at 4-4 in the eighth, Larry relieved Roger Craig. He set Chicago on its ear. In the Los Angeles half Hodges homered, and Sherry protected the advantage. The Series stood Los Angeles 3, Chicago 1. However, the White Sox bounced back to take the fifth in a tight 1-0 struggle.

Now in the sixth game, Sherry was once again making the long march in from the bullpen.

While Al Smith did a tantalizing dance off first base, Bubba Phillips, the next Chicago hitter, greeted Sherry with a sharp single. Jim McAnany struck out. But Earl Torgeson, a pinch hitter, walked. Two down. The bases filled. Luis Aparicio, always dangerous, at the plate. Larry was in deep trouble.

Sherry bore down. He nailed Aparicio on a pop fly. That was Chicago's last threat. Sherry set the remaining batters down like tenpins, hurling shutout balls for the next five innings, chalking up his second triumph of the Series.

The Dodgers had brought the world championship to Los Angeles. And the toast of California was none other than Larry Sherry, who less than four months earlier had yet to appear in his first big-league ball game!

LARRY SHERRY WINS SERIES FINALE The Dodger pitcher hurls 5⅔ innings of shutout ball, bringing first world championship to Los Angeles.

Mazeroski homers to win it for the Bucs.

Forbes Field, Pittsburgh, October 13, 1960

It came with such suddenness, rocketing off the bat of second baseman Bill Mazeroski of the Pirates, crashing over the head of Yogi Berra and over the left field wall, setting off a demonstration in downtown Pittsburgh that hadn't been seen since World War II ended!

Bill Mazeroski, known as the best in the business at making a double play, but not an especially tough hitter, had won the seventh game of the 1960 World Series with a dramatic home run.

It had been one of the wildest Series in years, the mighty Yankees of Mickey Mantle, Roger Maris, Yogi Berra, Moose Skowron against the tough, talented Pittsburgh Pirates of Roberto Clemente, Bill Virdon, Vernon Law, Bob Friend, and Dick Stuart—the man known as Dr. Strangeglove for the many holes in his first baseman's mitt.

The Yankees—who hadn't been in Pittsburgh since their Murderers' Row of 1927 had wiped out the Pirates 4-0—in this Series had beaten the Pirates 16-3, 10-0, and 12-0, in an awesome display of power. One Mantle homer, hit off Fred Green, was seen leaving the universe about two miles over the top of Forbes Field. But finally, it came down to game seven, the teams tied three each, and the score 9-9, as Ralph Terry, a long, thin righthander, was coming in to pitch against Mazeroski.

The Yankees had shocked the Pirates by tying the score in the top of the ninth at 9-9, and now most fans expected the Pirates to roll over and die.

No corpse ever proved more sprightly. Terry started the inning by throwing a ball to Mazeroski. The second baseman dug his heels a little deeper into the dirt around home plate, pumped his bat twice, and waited for the pitch. It was high and tight, a good pitch for Terry, a better one for Mazeroski as he timed it just right and exploded. The ball went back toward the wall, and Yogi Berra, who was finishing his career as an outfielder after so many great years as a catcher, floated back a step or two and then stopped.

The ball went over the wall, and Mazeroski had given the Pirates the championship of the world.

FANS HAIL MAZEROSKI AS HE HEADS FOR HOME Pittsburgh fans rush on to field to greet Pirates second baseman Bill Mazeroski. Mazeroski walloped a 400-foot, ninth-inning, Series-winning home run.

Roger Maris hits 61st home run of season.

Yankee Stadium, New York, October 1, 1961

There was nobody on base. No pennant hung in the balance. The count was not three and two, nor was it even the ninth inning. But everybody in the park was sitting on the edge of his seat, tensed as if a world championship hung on every pitch. For Roger Maris was at bat, needing just one more home run to become the all-time home run champion. It was the final game of the season, and Maris was still 360 feet from baseball immortality.

Tracy Stallard, Boston righthander, was on the mound. Only a rookie, he was shutting out the mighty Bronx Bombers. Now, in the fourth inning, it was a scoreless tie. Some pitchers might have walked Maris; but Stallard was determined not to put the winning run on base—if he could help it.

The pitch came in—over the plate—and Roger made the most of it. Swinging with all his strength, Maris sent a screaming drive towards the right field stands. As it cleared the fence, the crowd went wild!

No other Yankee that day could manage to score against Stallard's baffling pitches. No matter, for Maris' mighty blast had won the game, 1-0. It also gave him the RBI crown for the season (142) and the Runs Scored title (132, tied with teammate Mickey Mantle).

But the biggest thing that home run did was to break the season home run record of the immortal Babe Ruth. Thirty-four years before, the fabulous Babe had set the most celebrated of his many records by hitting the titanic total of 60 homers in one season. Since then, all the top sluggers of the game—players such as Ted Williams, Stan Musial, Joe DiMaggio, Hank Greenberg, and Jimmy Foxx—had striven in vain to match that total. All had fallen short.

Certainly back in May nobody had dreamed that Roger might do it. As late as May 16th, when the Yankees had played 27 games, he had only three home runs to his credit. Then he caught fire and started hitting four-baggers with almost unbelievable regularity. In the next 68 ball games, he hit 37 homers. During the last two months of the season, pitchers had desperately tried to avoid giving him decent pitches to swing at. This slowed him down; but still, in mid-August, he had a record-tying string of seven homers in six games.

From then on the pressure of publicity and the dwindling days left on the calendar never let up. Roger got number 50 on August 22, the earliest any player had ever reached 50. In the 154th game (which was the length of the schedule when Ruth set his mark), Maris hit his 59th. The record-tying 60th came six days later. The stage was set for Maris' big moment. It came on the very last day of the season!

MARIS HITS 61st HOME RUN This is the swing that made baseball history. Maris waits for the pitch, then swings with all his might. After following through, he drops bat and watches the ball soar into the right field stands.

Koufax strikes out 15 Yankees for record.

Yankee Stadium, New York, October 2, 1963

The capacity crowd of 69,000 in Yankee Stadium had come to see a pitching duel between lefthanders Whitey Ford of the Yanks and Sandy Koufax of the Dodgers. It was the 1963 opener.

What they witnessed was one of the most brilliant Series efforts of all time. Koufax, a 25-game winner during the regular 1963 campaign, made the powerful Bombers swing at thin air. The fireballing southpaw had his crackling curve, his bewildering fastball, and his mysterious floater working to perfection. During the regular season, Sandy had fanned 306 batters for a National League record. But no one quite expected him to mow down the American League kingpins in the same fashion.

Right at the start Koufax showed he meant business. He struck out Tony Kubek, Bobby Richardson, and Tom Tresh in the first inning. In the second, he whiffed Mickey Mantle and Roger Maris in order, and Elston Howard, the Yankee catcher, ended Sandy's strikeout string with a feeble pop foul.

Meanwhile the Dodgers built up an impressive lead. In the second stanza, Johnny Roseboro slammed a home run with two on. Another tally came across later to put the L.A. team in front by 4-0. In the third, it became 5-0.

But Koufax did not relax. In the fourth, he struck out the top three of the Yankee batting order. In the fifth, he fanned Mantle again. But with two out in the fifth, suddenly the Yanks got moving, and rattled off three hits in a row to fill the bases. That brought up Lopez, pinch-hitting for Ford. But he was no match for Sandy. Hector went down swinging, Koufax's 11th victim. Koufax was now only three short of the record.

In the eighth, Kubek beat out a hit. Richardson struck out for the third time. But Tresh followed with a home run, cutting the Dodger edge to 5-2.

It was the ninth. The Dodger southpaw needed but one more strikeout to engrave his name in the hall of records. With one out, Pepitone rifled a single to right. Clete Boyer followed with a towering drive that Willie Davis in center field just managed to overhaul. Manager Ralph Hauk sent up a pinch hitter for Steve Hamilton, his relief pitcher. Harry Bright, a righthanded batsman with good power and a good eye, came to the plate. Koufax and Roseboro went into a brief huddle.

Then Sandy poured two strikes past the pinch hitter. Could he make it number 15 in the strikeout column? He put everything he had on the next pitch. Bright swung—*and missed!*

The Dodgers had won the opening game. Buoyed by this great start, they were to take the next three for a World Series sweep. And Koufax had his record, striking out 15 batters, in a World Series game.

SANDY KOUFAX FANS 15 BATTERS IN WORLD SERIES GAME.

Jim Bunning pitches perfect game.

Shea Stadium, New York, June 21, 1964

The New York Mets were an expansion team used to losing steadily. In 1962, in their first season, they had lost 120 games. They managed to lose 111 in their second season. In their third season, in 1964, under manager Casey Stengel, they were moving along smartly at a pace that would get them only 109 losses. These boys almost always lost, but they almost always hit.

Only Sandy Koufax had been able to no-hit them in more than two seasons, turning the feat on June 30, 1962.

On June 21, 1964, Jim Bunning was the scheduled starter for the Philadelphia Phillies against the Mets. Bunning had been a big winner with the Detroit Tigers before coming over to the Phillies. He had also pitched a no-hitter on July 20, 1958 against the Red Sox at Fenway Park, a very hard task in a park famous for its short wall in left field, a wall known as the Green Monster. Now Bunning was going against the Mets.

What made the day exceptional was this: Jim Bunning, father of eight children, was pitching on Father's Day in New York with his wife and six of his children in attendance. He had asked for good seats for his family, and the Mets had come up with some seats in the far corner of the stadium. Bunning, a fiery competitor under any circumstances, was angered by what he considered "bush" treatment by the Mets. He vowed to make them pay the price on the field.

He started out with a rising fastball, a hard curve, and pinpoint control as he set the Mets down quickly in the first three innings—no runs, no hits, no walks, no errors.

During the fourth, the fifth, the sixth, and the seventh innings, no Met hitter reached first base.

The crowd began to pull for Bunning. All of a sudden, he was a hero even though he was an opponent. Everybody wanted to witness this historic event. After all, there had been only three perfect games in regular season play in all baseball history—by Cy Young in 1904, by Addie Joss in 1908, and by Charles Robertson in 1922.

The Mets went down in order in the eighth. Then the first two hitters went easily in the ninth. Bunning was one out away from history.

The batter was Johnny Stephenson, a rookie lefthanded hitter. Bunning got two quick strikes on him. Then Stephenson, fighting hard to avoid being the 27th out, fouled off five straight curves. He wanted a fastball to hit. Bunning went with his curve ball against the young, inexperienced hitter. Bunning went into his motion, pumped, kicked, and fired another curve ball. Stephenson took a mighty rip. Strike three swinging! Twenty-seven Mets up, 27 down, a perfect game! And Bunning's second no-hitter!

"Next time I pitch here," he said, "I hope I have better seats for my family."

JIM BUNNING HURLS PERFECT NINE-INNING GAME. The redoubtable righthander pitches nine innings of flawless ball, the first time feat was performed in a regular season in 42 years.

Gibson beats the Yanks for the championship.

Busch Stadium, St. Louis, October 14, 1964

As a youngster, he was thin and sickly. For the first four months of his life, he was given daily sun treatments to help subdue a severe case of rickets. One side of his chest was lower than the other; his bones had failed to develop properly.

"He was born sick," says Bob's mother, "and he got sicker. He had rickets, hay fever, asthma, pneumonia, and a rheumatic heart. I never thought he's make it."

But last season, at the age of 28, Gibson, a 6-foot-1, 195-pounder made it for real. The pennant race had been tight. The Cards came from behind to overhaul the Phillies and the Reds to win the National League pennant on the final day. In that exciting spurt it was Gibson's 19 victories that were telling.

If the pennant victory was hard-fought, the World Series loomed as even a more difficult assignment. The Yankees, smarting from their shellacking at the hands of the Los Angeles Dodgers the previous year, were seeking to regain the world title. And their big guns were ready: Mickey Mantle, Roger Maris, Elston Howard, Joe Pepitone.

The Cards were exhausted from the pressure-packed climax of the pennant race. Among the weariest of the weary was Bob Gibson.

He had pitched twice in the final three days of the campaign. In his initial World Series assignment, the second game, Gibson was not at his best. The Yanks eased to an 8-3 triumph to draw even with one game apiece.

With the Series count again deadlocked 2-2, Cardinal manager Johnny Keane decided to go again with Gibson. This time, his right-handed ace responded with a 5-2 victory, which dragged out to 10 innings, during which he struck out 13 batters.

In the sixth game, the Yanks bounced back to win 8-3. All was in deadlock now, and number 7 coming up, was life or death.

Keane called on Gibson again—this time with only two days rest. Bob's opponent was Mel Stottlemyre, New York's outstanding rookie righthander.

For three innings, the pitchers hurled almost flawless balls. But in the fourth the Cards scored three runs; and in the fifth, they tallied three more to take a 6-0 lead.

But Gibson, taking deep breaths between almost every pitch, was starting to tire. In the sixth, the Yanks got to him for three runs, on singles by Bobby Richardson and Roger Maris, and Mantle's home run into the left field stands.

At this point, Keane conferred with Gibson, and then decided to leave him in. In the seventh frame, St. Louis boosted its margin to 7-3.

Then came the fateful ninth. Tom Tresh struck out. Clete Boyer homered. Pinch hitter John Blanchard fanned for the second out, and then Phil Linz cut the Cards' lead to two runs, by hammering another four-bagger into the left field seats.

Two pitchers were warming up in the Cards' bullpen. But Keane decided to stay with his starting pitcher for one more batter. Bobby Richardson approached the plate. Mantle and Maris were ominously standing by. But those redoubtable sluggers never got a chance, for Gibson with the courage and talent that goes to make a champion, caused Richardson to lift an easy pop fly, gathered in effortlessly by second baseman Maxvill.

In the final set-to, Bob Gibson had fanned nine batters, lifting his total for the series to 31—a post-season whiffing record. He had brought the first world's title to St. Louis in 18 years.

GIBSON EXCELS IN SERIES FINALE
The Cardinal mainstay holds out for the full nine innings to bring the world championship to St. Louis.

Fat boy Lolich comes through.

Busch Stadium, St. Louis, October 10, 1968

He was an unlikely looking pitcher. Just a fat guy with a big beer belly who looked more like a truck driver playing softball on a Sunday afternoon.

But looks were deceiving in the case of Mickey Lolich, the crafty lefthander of the Detroit Tigers. Especially on October 10, 1968 in St. Louis in the seventh game of the World Series. That was the year Lolich's teammate, Denny McLain, had gotten all the attention around Detroit, for winning 31 games.

Now it was World Series time. Lolich had won game two of the Series, then game five, and now was going in game seven against Bob Gibson, one of the great money pitchers of all time.

The Cardinals had led three games to one in the Series. Then the tide shifted when Lou Brock failed to slide on a play at home, and was called out.

Suddenly, the Tigers revived, fought back, and now were even. It was three each. Lolich vs. Gibson—the smart, chubby lefthander against the explosive athletically trim righthander of the Cardinals.

Not many people figured Lolich would best Gibson in so big a game. Not many people figured on Lolich's heart and on his smarts. The lefthander was also suffering from an infection, and he was not up to par as he took the mound against the Cards. But as he got into a pitching groove, his energy seemed to come back. He got through six innings without any damage.

Then Detroit got a break. Curt Flood, one of the best defensive outfielders in the game, lost Jim Northrup's fly ball in a background of the white shirts in the stands. There were two men on base, when the ball fell behind Flood for a triple. Both runners came home, and the Tigers soon had three runs on the scoreboard. Another Detroit run made it 4-0 in the ninth. Mike Shannon belted a homer in the St. Louis ninth to make the final score 4-1.

Mickey Lolich, the fat boy from Detroit, had won three games and led the Tigers to an upset victory. Lolich was an unemotional sort. When it was over, he simply said, "I'm just glad the season is finished, so I can go out in the woods and ride my bike again."

Aaron passes The Babe's record.

Atlanta Stadium, April 8, 1974

It was a record that would never be broken. That is what they said after Babe Ruth hit his 714th home run, on a three home run day in Pittsburgh for the Braves, at the end of his brilliant career following his Yankee days for the Yankee dollar.

He had smashed 60 homers in 1927 and that record lasted until 1961, when Roger Maris passed it with 61. But that was in an expanded season, and Ford Frick, the commissioner of baseball, had ruled the Maris record would forever be tarnished with an asterisk.

Now Aaron was closing in on The Babe. Suddenly, he seemed to be hitting homers in huge amounts, 44 homers (his uniform number) on four separate occasions, 47 in 1971 at age 37, and 40 homers in 1973 at age 39. He had 713 as he closed the 1973 season.

In 1974, the Atlanta Braves wanted him to break the record at home. Commissioner Bowie Kuhn—a big buttinsky—stepped in and ordered The Hammer to nail the last two on the road—if he could.

Aaron opened in Cincinnati with the Braves and hit number 714 off Jack Billingham. Then came the night of April 8, 1974, a packed house in Atlanta—53,775 fans—waiting for The Hammer to pass The Babe.

Veteran lefthander Al Downing was on the mound for the Dodgers. He threw a low fastball to Aaron and the great slugger reached down for the ball, lifted it toward the left field fence and the crowd held its breath. It sailed back, back and over the fence, being caught behind the wire by Tom House, a pitcher for the Braves.

Aaron had done it! He had made the great Babe number two. The fans rushed on the field to congratulate him, his teammates raced to the plate, his wife smothered him in kisses, the television screens across America lit up with repeats of the event. The Hammer had become number one of all time.

"Thank God, it's over," said Aaron. It was no easy chore chasing The Babe. It would be years before anybody would chase and challenge The Hammer.

Carlton Fisk hits homer to tie the Series.

Fenway Park, Boston, October 21, 1975

It was generally agreed by experts on the World Series scene in 1975 that the October Classic that year was the most exciting ever played. Cincinnati defeated Boston 4-3 with every contest being a spellbinder from the opening pitch to the closing out.

The Cincinnati Reds—the Big Red Machine—had a team loaded with stars: Pete Rose, Joe Morgan, Johnny Bench, and Tony Perez. And the Boston Red Sox were coming off a blazing pennant race battle with young stars of their own: Jim Rice, Fred Lynn, Rick Burleson, Carlton Fisk, and veteran Carl Yastrzemski.

The teams battled through the first five games with the Reds up three games to two as the Series returned to Boston.

Then came the sixth game. Many fans, sportswriters, and players called it the most exciting baseball game ever played. More miraculous plays were achieved in that encounter than might be recorded in several seasons.

Dwight Evans made a miraculous catch. Fred Lynn crashed into a wall. The Reds' Dave Concepcion made some plays at shortstop that left fans with mouths open and eyes unbelieving. But the game stayed tied through the 12th inning.

Rookie Pat Darcy was pitching for the Reds, and Fisk, who had been battered and beaten all game long by sliding Reds and his own wild pitches, came to bat. Extra innings games are rarely won by anything except mistakes, because the players have so little stamina left by the time the game drags on into the late hours. Catchers almost never do much at such a time because their energies have been sapped by catching, bending, tagging, and throwing as they direct the game from behind the plate.

Now came Darcy's pitch. Fisk, a strong, tall handsome man got the good wood on the fastball, and lofted it high and far toward the famed Green Monster. It wasn't a crashing blow, but it had height and distance. Fisk stood at home plate as the ball sailed away. He moved out a step from the plate and studied it. Up, up, and away, it went—like Superman. He began waving it to his right, trying with magic to push the ball into fair territory as it headed for the screen. It seemed to curve and then stop and straighten out. It was going, going, gone! A fair ball!

A home run! The Red Sox win 7-6, and the Series is tied at three games each.

In an instant, Fisk was leaping in the air, bouncing high at the plate, joyous with the triumph. He danced around the bases, and all Boston went wild! No matter that the Red Sox lost the next day, Fisk's homer is all any of them really remembered that year.

Jackson hits three homers in one Series game.

Yankee Stadium, New York, October 18, 1977

Reggie Jackson had always been an awesome slugger, capable of driving a ball as far as any man who ever swung a bat.

In 1969, in his second year with the Oakland A's, he had smashed 47 homers, making a stab at the Roger Maris record of 61, before illness and injury knocked him for a loop.

Now, in 1977, Jackson was playing his first season as the right fielder of the New York Yankees. He had belted 32 home runs as the Yankees rallied for the championship. Reggie had been the center of attraction all season, controversy swirling around his head like bugs at a picnic, after he signed for $3 million as a free agent.

The Yankees had won the league title in a dramatic finish against the Kansas City Royals. They led the Los Angeles Dodgers 3-2 in games on that Tuesday night in New York. Jackson had homered in game four of the Series. On his last at bat in game five, he homered again, his long, high drive crashing against the foul pole in right field in Dodger Stadium.

In game six, he performed an incredible feat. He hit a home run his first time up against starter Burt Hooton on the first pitch to him. Two homers in two at bats in a row. Now came another home run on the first pitch to him by relief pitcher Elias Sosa, three homers in a row, two in the same game. Now came the last at bat for Jackson. Only Babe Ruth, who had achieved the feat twice, had hit three home runs in one Series game. Nobody had ever hit three in a row on three pitches, nobody had ever hit four in a row over two games.

The pitcher was Charlie Hough, a tough knuckleballer for the Dodgers. Jackson stood at home plate, pumping that dark, brown bat of his. Hough stood on the mound studying the sign from his catcher. Hough threw knuckleballs almost exclusively so the sign-studying was mostly an act.

Here comes the knuckleball! Everybody in the park knew it. Whack! The sound could be heard all the way downtown as the ball shot off Reggie's bat, climbed high over the outfield, and crashed into an open section of the centerfield stands.

Three homers in one Series game! Four homers in a row! Five in the Series! An incredible performance by the man who was to become known as "The Candy Man" because the Reggie bar had been named after him. "Babe Ruth was great," said Jackson later, "I was only lucky."

Maybe so, but in no World Series before—and probably not in another for many years—would a slugger be that "lucky."

Yanks win playoff as Bucky Dent hits homer.

Fenway Park, Boston, October 2, 1978

It had everything—the Red Sox and the Yankees—the most heated rivalry in sports—the pennant riding on every pitch—the tight, noisy surroundings of old Fenway Park.

On October 2, 1978, a pleasant early fall afternoon, the Yankees and Red Sox battled head-to-head in a game many consider "the greatest game ever played."

The Red Sox had led the Yankees by 14 games on July 20th. Then the Yankees began winning, and the Red Sox began losing. Yankee manager Billy Martin was fired on July 24th, and Bob Lemon took over the next day.

The Yankees continued to win, and the Red Sox continued to lose. The race tightened. The Yanks swept a four-game series at Fenway over the weekend of September 10th. The teams were tied.

The Yanks soon moved ahead. But not for long. The Yankees were beaten on the final day of the regular season by the Cleveland Indians, and the Sox beat Toronto. The two teams were now tied after 162 games.

Now the season came down to one game in Fenway Park. With Mike Torrez, an ex-Yankee, pitching for Boston, and Ron Guidry pitching for the Yankees, the score stayed close with the Red Sox leading at 2-0 in the seventh.

Bucky Dent, a .243 hitter with only four homers, stood at home plate. The Yankees had two men on. He swung and fouled a ball off his leg, hopped around at the plate with his hot foot, and got back into the batter's box. The next pitch was high and inside. Dent swung and drove the ball on a high arc toward the short fence in left field, the well-known "Green Monster of Fenway." As Carl Yastrzemski looked up helplessly, the ball floated into the screen for three runs, and a 3-2 Yankee lead.

Reggie Jackson later homered and the Yankees took a 5-2 lead into the eighth inning. The Red Sox pushed two across in the eighth, as the fans screamed their heads off.

Now it was the ninth, two on for Boston, one out, slugger Jim Rice up, and Yastrzemski to follow. These were the two hitters Boston would want, could they pick any two from their lineup.

Rice hit a huge fly to right field. Now it was two out. The Red Sox had the winning run on first base, the tying run on third, and one of the great clutch hitters in the game at the plate!

Rich Gossage, who throws fastballs at 99 miles per hour, threw one of his best. It was inside and high on Yastrzemski. The Boston hero swung and lifted a foul ball to third. Graig Nettles camped under it, caught it, and the season was over.

The Yankees went on to defeat Kansas City in the American League championship series, and then beat the Dodgers four games to two in the World Series.

They were champions for the second year in a row after "the greatest game ever played." An unlikely slugger named Bucky Dent was the man of the hour.

THE WORLD SERIES—1978

The Yanks did it again!

The New York Yankees did it again in 1978. Won their 32nd pennant and 22nd world championship! The Yanks beat the Dodgers four games to two in one of the most exciting Series battles in years.

The Yankees had to overcome a 14-game deficit to catch the Boston Red Sox. They did it.

The Yanks then wiped out the Kansas City Royals for the American League pennant.

The Dodgers came from 6½ games back to catch and pass the Giants for their second straight pennant—only to go down to their second straight Series defeat. The Yankees have now beaten the Dodgers nine times in 11 Series matchups.

Bucky Dent, Reggie Jackson, Graig Nettles, Ron Guidry, and Catfish Hunter were the stars for the Yankees.

In Game One, Davey Lopes hit two homers, Dusty Baker hit one, and Tommy John handcuffed New York with his curves and fastballs. The Dodgers won 11-5.

Los Angeles won Game Two with a 4-3 victory, when rookie Bob Welch struck out Reggie Jackson, who swung vainly on a 3-2 pitch with the winning run on base.

In Game Three at Yankee Stadium, Ron Guidry pitched and Graig Nettles fielded sensationally to beat the Dodgers 5-1. Roy White homered for New York, and the Los Angeles lead was cut to 2-1 in games.

In Game Four, Lou Piniella singled in the 10th inning to break a 3-3 tie, and give the Yankees a 4-3 win. The Series was now tied 2-2.

The Yankees exploded in Game Five for a 12-2 victory as the Dodger defense fell apart.

The Series shifted back to Los Angeles for Game Six. The Yankees won again on a homer by Reggie Jackson and three hits each by rookie Brian Doyle and shortstop Bucky Dent.

Dent was voted the outstanding player of the Series. The Yanks had wrapped up the whole ball of wax and the world title with 4-2 in games.

RICH GOSSAGE

THE BATTING CHAMPIONS

A Roster of Leading Hitters

Rod Carew, Rogers Hornsby, and Stan Musial each won seven batting titles. They tied Honus Wagner, who won seven crowns in the modern era, and one in 1900, when the rules were slightly different. Ty Cobb, with 12 titles, stands at the top of the heap.

Carew has won out in six of the last seven seasons. The Minnesota star is only 33, so he might well win several more championships during his career.

	American League		National League	
1901	Nap Lajoie, Philadelphia	.422	Jesse Burkett, St. Louis	.382
1902	Ed Delahanty, Washington	.376	Ginger Beaumont, Pittsburgh	.357
1903	Nap Lajoie, Cleveland	.355	Honus Wagner, Pittsburgh	.355
1904	Nap Lajoie, Cleveland	.381	Honus Wagner, Pittsburgh	.349
1905	Elmer Flick, Cleveland	.306	Cy Seymour, Cincinnati	.377
1906	George Stone, St. Louis	.358	Honus Wagner, Pittsburgh	.339
1907	Ty Cobb, Detroit	.350	Honus Wagner, Pittsburgh	.350
1908	Ty Cobb, Detroit	.324	Honus Wagner, Pittsburgh	.354
1909	Ty Cobb, Detroit	.377	Honus Wagner, Pittsburgh	.339
1910	Ty Cobb, Detroit	.385	Sherwood Magee, Philadephia	.331

	American League		National League	
1911	Ty Cobb, Detroit	.420	Honus Wagner, Pittsburgh	.334
1912	Ty Cobb, Detroit	.410	Heinie Zimmerman, Chicago	.372
1913	Ty Cobb, Detroit	.390	Jake Daubert, Brooklyn	.350
1914	Ty Cobb, Detroit	.368	Jake Daubert, Brooklyn	.329
1915	Ty Cobb, Detroit	.370	Larry Doyle, New York	.320
1916	Tris Speaker, Cleveland	.386	Hal Chase, Cincinnati	.339
1917	Ty Cobb, Detroit	.383	Ed Roush, Cincinnati	.341
1918	Ty Cobb, Detroit	.382	Zack Wheat, Brooklyn	.335
1919	Ty Cobb, Detroit	.384	Ed Roush, Cincinnati	.321
1920	George Sisler, St. Louis	.407	Rogers Hornsby, St. Louis	.370
1921	Harry Heilmann, Detroit	.394	Rogers Hornsby, St. Louis	.397
1922	George Sisler, St. Louis	.420	Rogers Hornsby, St. Louis	.401
1923	Harry Heilmann, Detroit	.403	Rogers Hornsby, St. Louis	.384
1924	Babe Ruth, New York	.378	Rogers Hornsby, St. Louis	.424
1925	Harry Heilmann, Detroit	.393	Rogers Hornsby, St. Louis	.403
1926	Heinie Manush, Detroit	.377	Bubbles Hargrave, Cincinnati	.353
1927	Harry Heilmann, Detroit	.398	Paul Waner, Pittsburgh	.380
1928	Goose Goslin, Washington	.379	Rogers Hornsby, Boston	.387
1929	Lew Fonseca, Cleveland	.369	Lefty O'Doul, Philadelphia	.398
1930	Al Simmons, Philadelphia	.381	Bill Terry, New York	.401
1931	Al Simmons, Philadelphia	.390	Chick Hafey, St. Louis	.349
1932	Dale Alexander, Det.-Bos.	.390	Lefty O'Doul, Brooklyn	.368
1933	Jimmy Foxx, Philadelphia	.356	Chuck Klein, Philadelphia	.368
1934	Lou Gehrig, New York	.363	Paul Waner, Pittsburgh	.362
1935	Buddy Myer, Washington	.349	Arky Vaughan, Pittsburgh	.385
1936	Luke Appling, Chicago	.388	Paul Waner, Pittsburgh	.373
1937	Charlie Gehringer, Detroit	.371	Joe Medwick, St. Louis	.374
1938	Jimmy Foxx, Boston	.349	Ernie Lombardi, Cincinnati	.342
1939	Joe DiMaggio, New York	.381	Johnny Mize, St. Louis	.349
1940	Joe DiMaggio, New York	.352	Debs Garms, Pittsburgh	.355
1941	Ted Williams, Boston	.406	Pete Reiser, Brooklyn	.343
1942	Ted Williams, Boston	.356	Ernie Lombardi, Boston	.330
1943	Luke Appling, Chicago	.328	Stan Musial, St. Louis	.357
1944	Lou Boudreau, Cleveland	.327	Dixie Walker, Brooklyn	.357

	American League		**National League**	
1945	George Stirnweiss, New York	.309	Phil Cavarretta, Chicago	.355
1946	Mickey Vernon, Washington	.353	Stan Musial, St. Louis	.365
1947	Ted Williams, Boston	.343	Harry Walker, St. Louis-Phila.	.363
1948	Ted Williams, Boston	.369	Stan Musial, St. Louis	.376
1949	George Kell, Detroit	.343	Jackie Robinson, Brooklyn	.342
1950	Billy Goodman, Boston	.354	Stan Musial, St. Louis	.346
1951	Ferris Fain, Philadelphia	.344	Stan Musial, St. Louis	.355
1952	Ferris Fain, Philadelphia	.327	Stan Musial, St. Louis	.336
1953	Mickey Vernon, Washington	.337	Carl Furillo, Brooklyn	.344
1954	Bobby Avila, Cleveland	.341	Willie Mays, New York	.345
1955	Al Kaline, Detroit	.340	Richie Ashburn, Philadelphia	.338
1956	Mickey Mantle, New York	.353	Hank Aaron, Milwaukee	.328
1957	Ted Williams, Boston	.388	Stan Musial, St. Louis	.351
1958	Ted Williams, Boston	.328	Richie Ashburn, Philadelphia	.350
1959	Harvey Kuenn, Detroit	.353	Hank Aaron, Milwaukee	.355
1960	Pete Runnels, Boston	.320	Dick Groat, Pittsburgh	.325
1961	Norm Cash, Detroit	.361	Roberto Clemente, Pittsburgh	.351
1962	Pete Runnels, Boston	.326	Tommy Davis, Los Angeles	.346
1963	Carl Yastrzemski, Boston	.321	Tommy Davis, Los Angeles	.326
1964	Tony Oliva, Minnesota	.323	Roberto Clemente, Pittsburgh	.339
1965	Tony Oliva, Minnesota	.321	Roberto Clemente, Pittsburgh	.329
1966	Frank Robinson, Baltimore	.316	Matty Alou, Pittsburgh	.342
1967	Carl Yastrzemski, Boston	.326	Roberto Clemente, Pittsburgh	.357
1968	Carl Yastrzemski, Boston	.301	Pete Rose, Cincinnati	.335
1969	Rod Carew, Minnesota	.332	Pete Rose, Cincinnati	.348
1970	Alex Johnson, California	.329	Rico Carty, Atlanta	.366
1971	Tony Oliva, Minnesota	.337	Joe Torre, St. Louis	.363
1972	Rod Carew, Minnesota	.318	Billy Williams, Chicago	.333
1973	Rod Carew, Minnesota	.350	Pete Rose, Cincinnati	.338
1974	Rod Carew, Minnesot	.364	Ralph Garr, Atlanta	.353
1975	Rod Carew, Minnesota	.359	Bill Madlock, Chicago	.354
1976	George Brett, Kansas City	.333	Bill Madlock, Chicago	.339
1977	Rod Carew, Minnesota	.388	Dave Parker, Pittsburgh	.338
1978	Rod Carew, Minnesota	.333	Dave Parker, Pittsburgh	.334

THE THREE HUNDRED CLUB

Pitchers who have won more than 300 games.

Since baseball's records and pitching distances and rules were standardized at the turn of the century, only eight pitchers have won 300 games in their career. The last man to reach the mark was Early Wynn of the Cleveland Indians with his 300th victory in 1963 at age 43.

MEMBERS OF "THE 300 CLUB" ARE:

NAME	YEARS	WON	LOST
Grover Cleveland Alexander	20	373	208
Robert M. (Lefty) Grove	17	300	141
Walter P. Johnson	21	416	279
Christopher Mathewson	17	373	188
Edward S. Plank	17	325	190
Warren E. Spahn	21	363	245
Early Wynn	23	300	244
Denton True (Cy) Young	22	511	315

THE TWO HUNDRED CLUB

Another 52 pitchers have won 200 or more games. Jim Palmer, Steve Carlton, and Don Sutton joined this exclusive club in 1978. Phil Niekro, with 197 wins, will be the first to make it in 1979.

MEMBERS OF "THE 200 CLUB" ARE:

NAME	YEARS	WON	LOST
Charles A. (Chief) Bender	16	212	128
Mordecai (Three Finger) Brown	14	239	130
James P. Bunning	17	224	184
S. Lewis Burdette	18	203	144
Steven N. Carlton	14	207	149
Edward V. Cicotte	14	209	148
Wilbur A. Cooper	15	216	178
Stanley Covelski	14	216	142
George Dauss	15	218	184
Paul Derringer	15	223	212
Donald S. Drysdale	14	209	166
Urban C. Faber	20	254	212
Robert W. Feller	18	266	162
Fred L. Fitzsimmons	19	217	146
Edward C. (Whitey) Ford	16	236	106
Robert Gibson	17	251	174
Burleigh A. Grimes	19	270	212
Jesse J. Haines	19	210	158
Melvin L. Harder	20	223	186
Waite C. Hoyt	21	237	182
Carl O. Hubbell	16	253	154
James A. (Catfish) Hunter	14	222	157
Ferguson A. Jenkins	14	231	168
Samuel P. Jones	22	228	216

James L. Kaat	20	261	217
Robert G. Lemon	13	207	128
Michael S. Lolich	15	217	189
Theodore A. Lyons	21	260	230
Juan A. Marichal	16	243	142
Richard W. (Rube) Marquard	18	201	177
Carl W. Mays	15	203	128
Joseph J. McGinnity	10	247	142
George Mullin	14	228	193
Harold Newhouser	16	207	150
Louis N. (Bucky) Newson	20	211	222
James A. Palmer	13	215	116
Milton S. Pappas	17	209	164
Herbert J. Pennock	22	241	163
Gaylord Perry	17	267	206
James E. Perry	17	215	174
William W. Pierce	18	211	169
John Powell	17	248	258
John P. Quinn	23	247	216
Eppa Rixey	21	266	251
Robin E. Roberts	19	286	245
Charles H. Root	17	201	160
Charles H. (Red) Ruffing	22	273	225
G. Thomas Seaver	12	219	127
Donald H. Sutton	13	205	155
Luis Clemente Tiant	15	204	148
George Uhle	17	200	166
Earl O. Whitehill	17	218	186
Victor Willis	13	244	207

THE .400 HITTERS

Baseball's Biggest Bats

It is 38 years since Ted Williams finished the 1941 season with a mark of .406. Williams batted .388 in 1957. Rod Carew batted .388 in 1977. No one else has come close to these marks.

It is unlikely any hitter will ever again bat over .400. Modern baseball—with long trips, late night airplane flights, excessive travel, and night games—is too demanding on the player.

Only seven hitters in modern Major League history have batted .400 for a full season. Two, Ty Cobb and Rogers Hornsby, were able to pull this feat three times.

The other five men who batted over .400 were Joe Jackson, George Sisler, Harry Heilmann, Bill Terry, and Ted Williams.

Williams was batting .401 on the last day of the 1941 season. Manager Joe Cronin suggested Ted sit out the final doubleheader and protect his average. Williams refused. Like a true champion, he played, raised his average to .406 and set a mark that has not been approached in nearly four decades.

Here is the exclusive .400 club:

1911	Joe Jackson	Cleveland Indians	.408
1911	Ty Cobb	Detroit Tigers	.420
1912	Ty Cobb	Detroit Tigers	.410
1920	George Sisler	St. Louis Browns	.407
1922	Ty Cobb	Detroit Tigers	.401
1922	George Sisler	St. Louis Browns	.420
1922	Rogers Hornsby	St. Louis Cardinals	.401
1923	Harry Heilmann	Detroit Tigers	.403
1924	Rogers Hornsby	St. Louis Cardinals	.424
1925	Rogers Hornsby	St. Louis Cardinals	.403
1930	Bill Terry	New York Giants	.401
1941	Ted Williams	Boston Red Sox	.406

THE HOME RUN CHAMPIONS

The Game's Biggest Bombers

Roger Maris holds baseball's single-season home run record. He hit 61 homers in 1961 in a 162-game season. That broke Babe Ruth's mark of 60 homers made in a 154-game season in 1927.

The Babe won the home run crown 10 separate times, and has tied for it two other times: once in 1918, he tied Clarence Walker with 11 homers; and again in 1931, with 46 homers, when he was tied with Lou Gehrig.

Ruth hit 59 homers in 1921 to set a record that year. He passed his own mark in 1927. No other hitter had ever hit 59 in a season.

Jimmy Foxx of the A's had 58 in 1932, and Hank Greenberg of the Tigers had 58 in 1938. The National League mark is 56 by Hack Wilson of the Cubs in 1930.

Hank Aaron holds the career mark for homers with 755 home runs in 23 seasons.

Jim Rice of Boston hit 46 homers to win the home run crown in 1978 in the American League. George Foster hit 40 to win in the National League.

	American League		**National League**	
1901	Nap Lajoie, Philadelphia	13	Sam Crawford, Cincinnati	16
1902	Ralph Seybold, Philadelphia	16	Tom Leach, Pittsburgh	6
1903	John Freeman, Boston	13	Jimmy Sheckard, Brooklyn	9
1904	Harry Davis, Philadelphia	10	Harry Lumley, Brooklyn	9
1905	Harry Davis, Philadelphia	8	Fred Odwell, Cincinnati	9
1906	Harry Davis, Philadelphia	12	Tim Jordan, Brooklyn	12
1907	Harry Davis, Philadelphia	8	Dave Brain, Boston	10
1908	Sam Crawford, Detroit	7	Tim Jordan, Brooklyn	10
1909	Ty Cobb, Detroit	9	John Murray, New York	7
1910	Jake Stahl, Boston	10	Fred Beck, Boston	10
			Frank Schulte, Chicago	10
1911	Frank Baker, Philadelphia	9	Frank Schulte, Chicago	21
1912	Frank Baker, Philadelphia	10	Henie Zimmerman, Chicago	14
1913	Frank Baker, Philadelphia	12	Cactus Cravath, Philadelphia	19
1914	Frank Baker, Philadelphia	8	Cactus Cravath, Philadelphia	19
1915	Bob Roth, Chicago-Cleveland	7	Cactus Cravath, Philadelphia	24
1916	Wallie Pipp, New York	12	Dave Roberston, New York	12
			Fred Williams, Chicago	12
1917	Wallie Pipp, New York	9	Cactus Cravath, Philadelphia	12
			Dave Robertson, New York	12
1918	C.W. Walker, Philadelphia	11	Cactus Cravath, Philadelphia	8
	Babe Ruth, Boston	11		
1919	Babe Ruth, Boston	29	Cactus Cravath, Philadelphia	12
1920	Babe Ruth, New York	54	Fred Williams, Philadelphia	15
1921	Babe Ruth, New York	59	George Kelly, New York	23
1922	Ken Williams, St. Louis	39	Rogers Hornsby, St. Louis	42
1923	Babe Ruth, New York	41	Fred Williams, Philadelphia	41
1924	Babe Ruth, New York	46	Jacques Fournier, Brooklyn	27
1925	Bob Meusel, New York	33	Rogers Hornsby, St. Louis	39
1926	Babe Ruth, New York	47	Hack Wilson, Chicago	21
1927	Babe Ruth, New York	60	Hack Wilson, Chicago	30
			Fred Williams, Philadelphia	30
1928	Babe Ruth, New York	54	Jim Bottomley, St. Louis	31
			Hack Wilson, Chicago	31
1929	Babe Ruth, New York	46	Chas. Klein, Philadelphia	43

	American League		National League	
1930	Babe Ruth, New York	49	Hack Wilson, Chicago	56
1931	Babe Ruth, New York	46	Chas. Klein, Philadelphia	31
	Lou Gehrig, New York	46		
1932	Jimmy Foxx, Philadelphia	58	Chas. Klein, Philadelphia	38
			Mel Ott, New York	38
1933	Jimmy Foxx, Philadelphia	48	Chas. Klein, Philadelphia	38
1934	Lou Gehrig, New York	49	Jim Collins, St. Louis	35
			Mel Ott, New York	35
1935	Hank Greenberg, Detroit	36	Wallie Berger, Boston	34
	Jimmy Foxx, Philadephia	36		
1936	Lou Gehrig, New York	49	Mel Ott, New York	33
1937	Joe DiMaggio, New York	46	Mel Ott, New York	31
			Joe Medwick, St. Louis	31
1938	Hank Greenberg, Detroit	58	Mel Ott, New York	36
1939	Jimmy Foxx, Boston	35	John Mize, St. Louis	28
1940	Hank Greenberg, Detroit	41	John Mize, St. Louis	43
1941	Ted Williams, Boston	37	Dolph Camilli, Brooklyn	34
1942	Ted Williams, Boston	36	Mel Ott, New York	30
1943	Rudy York, Detroit	34	William Nicholson, Chicago	29
1944	Nick Etten, New York	22	William Nicholson, Chicago	33
1945	Vernon Stephens, St. Louis	24	Thomas Holmes, Boston	28
1946	Hank Greenberg, Detroit	44	Ralph Kiner, Pittsburgh	23
1947	Ted Williams, Boston	32	Ralph Kiner, Pittsburgh	51
			John Mize, New York	51
1948	Joe DiMaggio, New York	39	Ralph Kiner, Pittsburgh	40
			John Mize, New York	40
1949	Ted Williams, Boston	43	Ralph Kiner, Pittsburgh	54
1950	Al Rosen, Cleveland	37	Ralph Kiner, Pittsburgh	47
1951	Gus Zernial, Chicago-Phila.	33	Ralph Kiner, Pittsburgh	42
1952	Larry Doby, Cleveland	32	Hank Sauer, Chicago	37
			Ralph Kiner, Pittsburgh	37
1953	Al Rosen, Cleveland	43	Ed Mathews, Milwaukee	47
1954	Larry Doby, Cleveland	32	Ted Kluszewski, Cincinnati	49
1955	Mickey Mantle, New York	37	Willie Mays, New York	51
1956	Mickey Mantle, New York	52	Duke Snider, Brooklyn	43

	American League		**National League**	
1957	Roy Sievers, Washington	42	Hank Aaron, Milwaukee	44
1958	Mickey Mantle, New York	42	Ernie Banks, Chicago	47
1959	Rocky Colavito, Cleveland	42	Ed Mathews, Milwaukee	46
	Harmon Killebrew, Washington	42		
1960	Mickey Mantle, New York	40	Ernie Banks, Chicago	41
1961	Roger Maris, New York	61	Orlando Cepeda, San Francisco	46
1962	Harmon Killebrew, Minnesota	48	Willie Mays, San Francisco	49
1963	Harmon Killebrew, Minnesota	45	Hank Aaron, Milwaukee	44
1964	Harmon Killebrew, Minnesota	49	Willie Mays, San Francisco	47
1965	Tony Conigliaro, Boston	32	Willie Mays, San Francisco	52
1966	Frank Robinson, Baltimore	49	Hank Aaron, Atlanta	44
1967	Harmon Killebrew, Minnesota	44	Hank Aaron, Atlanta	39
	Carl Yastrzemski, Boston	44		
1968	Frank Howard, Washington	44	Willie McCovey, San Francisco	36
1969	Harmon Killebrew, Minnesota	49	Willie McCovey, San Francisco	45
1970	Frank Howard, Washington	44	Johnny Bench, Cincinnati	45
1971	Bill Melton, Chicago	33	Willie Stargell, Pittsburgh	48
1972	Dick Allen, Chicago	37	Johnny Bench, Cincinnati	40
1973	Reggie Jackson, Oakland	32	Willie Stargell, Pittsburgh	44
1974	Dick Allen, Chicago	32	Mike Schmidt, Philadelphia	36
1975	Reggie Jackson, Oakland	36	Mike Schmidt, Philadelphia	38
	George Scott, Milwaukee	36		
1976	Graig Nettles, New York	32	Mike Schmidt, Philadelphia	38
1977	Jim Rice, Boston	39	George Foster, Cincinnati	52
1978	Jim Rice, Boston	46	George Foster, Cincinnati	40

JACKIE ROBINSON This Hall of Famer was the first Negro to play in major leagues—with Brooklyn Dodgers from 1947 through 1956.

THE PITCHING CHAMPIONS

Earned Run Average

	National League		*American League*	
1913	Christy Mathewson, New York	2.06	Walter Johnson, Washington	1.14
1914	Bill Doak, St. Louis	1.72	Dutch Leonard, Boston	1.01
1915	Grover Alexander, Philadelphia	1.22	Joe Wood, Boston	1.49
1916	Grover Alexander, Philadelphia	1.55	Babe Ruth, Boston	1.75
1917	Grover Alexander, Philadelphia	1.85	Ed Cicotte, Chicago	1.53
1918	Hippo Vaughn, Chicago	1.74	Walter Johnson, Washington	1.28
1919	Grover Alexander, Chicago	1.72	Walter Johnson, Washington	1.49
1920	Grover Alexander, Chicago	1.91	Bob Shawkey, New York	2.46
1921	Bill Doak, St. Louis	2.58	Red Faber, Chicago	2.48
1922	Rosy Ryan, New York	3.00	Red Faber, Chicago	2.81
1923	Dolf Luque, Cincinnati	1.93	Stan Covelski, Cleveland	2.76
1924	Dazzy Vance, Brooklyn	2.16	Walter Johnson, Washington	2.72
1925	Dolf Luque, Cincinnati	2.63	Stan Covelski, Cleveland	2.84
1926	Ray Kremer, Pittsburgh	2.61	Lefty Grove, Philadelphia	2.51
1927	Ray Kremer, Pittsburgh	2.47	Wilcy Moore, New York	2.28
1928	Dazzy Vance, Brooklyn	2.09	Garland Braxton, Washington	2.52
1929	Bill Walker, New York	3.08	Lefty Grove, Philadelphia	2.82
1930	Dazzy Vance, Brooklyn	2.61	Lefty Grove, Philadelphia	2.54
1931	Bill Walker, New York	2.26	Lefty Grove, Philadelphia	2.05
1932	Lon Warneke, Chicago	2.37	Lefty Grove, Philadelphia	2.84
1933	Carl Hubbell, New York	1.66	Monte Pearson, Cleveland	2.33
1934	Carl Hubbell, New York	2.30	Lefty Gomez, New York	2.33
1935	Cy Blanton, Pittsburgh	2.59	Lefty Grove, Boston	2.70
1936	Carl Hubbell, New York	2.31	Lefty Grove, Boston	2.81
1937	Jim Turner, Boston	2.38	Lefty Gomez, New York	2.33
1938	Bill Lee, Chicago	2.66	Lefty Grove, Boston	3.07
1939	Bucky Walters, Cincinnati	2.29	Lefty Grove, Boston	2.54
1940	Bucky Walters, Cincinnati	2.48	Bob Feller, Cleveland	2.62
1941	Elmer Riddle, Cincinnati	2.24	Thornton Lee, Chicago	2.27
1942	Mort Cooper, St. Louis	1.77	Ted Lyons, Chicago	2.10

	National League		**American League**	
1943	Howard Pollet, St. Louis	1.75	Spud Chandler, New York	1.64
1944	Ed Heusser, Cincinnati	2.38	Dizzy Trout, Detroit	2.12
1945	Hank Borowy, Chicago	2.14	Hal Newhouser, Detroit	1.81
1946	Howard Pollet, St. Louis	2.10	Hal Newhouser, Detroit	1.94
1947	Warren Spahn, Boston	2.33	Spud Chandler, New York	2.46
1948	Hal Brecheen, St. Louis	2.24	Gene Beardon, Cleveland	2.43
1949	Dave Koslo, New York	2.50	Mel Parnell, Boston	2.78
1950	Jim Hearn, St. Louis-New York	2.49	Early Wynn, Cleveland	3.20
1951	Chet Nichols, Boston	2.88	Sol Rogavin, Detroit-Chicago	2.78
1952	Hoyt Wilhelm, New York	2.43	Allie Reynolds, New York	2.07
1953	Warren Spahn, Milwaukee	2.10	Eddie Lopat, New York	2.43
1954	John Antonelli, New York	2.29	Mike Garcia, Cleveland	2.64
1955	Bob Friend, Pittsburgh	2.84	Billy Pierce, Chicago	1.97
1956	Lew Burdette, Milwaukee	2.71	Whitey Ford, New York	2.47
1957	John Podres, Brooklyn	2.66	Bobby Shantz, New York	2.45
1958	Stu Miller, San Francisco	2.47	Whitey Ford, New York	2.01
1959	Sam Jones, San Francisco	2.82	Hoyt Wilhelm, Baltimore	2.19
1960	Mike McCormick, San Francisco	2.70	Frank Baumann, Chicago	2.68
1961	Warren Spahn, Milwaukee	3.01	Dick Donovan, Washington	2.40
1962	Sandy Koufax, Los Angeles	2.54	Hank Aguirre, Detroit	2.21
1963	Sandy Koufax, Los Angeles	1.88	Gary Peters, Chicago	2.33
1964	Sandy Koufax, Los Angeles	1.74	Dean Chance, Los Angeles	1.65
1965	Sandy Koufax, Los Angeles	2.04	Sam McDowell, Cleveland	2.18
1966	Sandy Koufax, Los Angeles	1.73	Gary Peters, Chicago	1.98
1967	Phil Niekro, Atlanta	1.87	Joel Horlen, Chicago	2.06
1968	Bob Gibson, St. Louis	1.12	Luis Tiant, Cleveland	1.60
1969	Juan Marichal, San Francisco	2.10	Dick Bosman, Washington	2.19
1970	Tom Seaver, New York	2.81	Diego Segui, Oakland	2.56
1971	Tom Seaver, New York	1.76	Vida Blue, Oakland	1.82
1972	Steve Carlton, Philadelphia	1.98	Luis Tiant, Boston	1.91
1973	Tom Seaver, New York	2.08	Jim Palmer, Baltimore	2.40
1974	Buzz Capra, Atlanta	2.28	Catfish Hunter, Oakland	2.49
1975	Randy Jones, San Diego	2.24	Jim Palmer, Baltimore	2.09
1976	John Denny, St. Louis	2.52	Mark Fidrych, Detroit	2.34
1977	John Candelaria, Pittsburgh	2.34	Frank Tanana, California	2.54
1978	Gaylord Perry, San Diego	2.73	Ron Guidry, New York	1.74

THE BALL PARKS

CITY	PARK	CAPACITY

National League

Atlanta	Atlanta-Fulton County Stadium	52,194
Chicago	Wrigley Field	37,741
Cincinnati	Riverfront Stadium	51,880
Houston	Astrodome	45,000
Los Angeles	Dodger Stadium	56,000
Montreal	Olympic Stadium	59,511
New York	Shea Stadium	55,300
Philadelphia	Veterans Stadium	58,651
Pittsburgh	Three Rivers Stadium	50,230
St. Louis	Busch Memorial Stadium	50,222
San Diego	San Diego Stadium	48,443
San Francisco	Candlestick Park	58,000

American League

Baltimore	Memorial Stadium	52,860
Boston	Fenway Park	33,502
California	Anaheim Stadium	43,250
Chicago	Comiskey Park	44,492
Cleveland	Cleveland Stadium	76,713
Detroit	Tiger Stadium	53,676
Kansas City	Royals Stadium	40,762
Milwaukee	County Stadium	54,187
Minnesota	Metropolitan Stadium	45,919
New York	Yankee Stadium	57,545
Oakland	Oakland Coliseum	50,000
Seattle	The Kingdome	59,059
Texas	Arlington Stadium	41,097
Toronto	Exhibition Stadium	43,737

THE WORLD CHAMPIONS

Roster of Series Winners

The best team in baseball history, the New York Yankees, did it again in 1978 with its 22nd world championship and 32nd pennant. They beat the Dodgers four games to two in one of the most exciting Series battles ever.

The Yankees had to overcome a 14-game deficit to catch the Boston Red Sox. They did it, finally, in a one-game playoff for the division title when Bucky Dent, their fine-fielding shortstop, lofted a three-run homer off the screen at Fenway Park to send Mike Torrez and the Red Sox to defeat. Reggie Jackson, known as Mr. October, contributed the key run with a long homer.

The Yankees then wiped out the Kansas City Royals for the American League pennant.

The Dodgers came from six-and-one-half games back to catch and pass the Giants for their second straight pennant, only to go down to their second straight Series defeat.

Bucky Dent, Reggie Jackson, Graig Nettles, Ron Guidry, and Catfish Hunter were the Series stars for the Yankees.

The Yankees had not won a World Series since 1962. But they came back in 1977, and again in 1978 to win back-to-back titles. The Yankees now have beaten the Dodgers nine times in 11 Series matchups.

YEAR	NATIONAL LEAGUE	AMERICAN LEAGUE	W.S. WINNER	SCORE
1903	Pittsburgh	Boston	Boston, A.L.	5-3
1905	New York	Philadelphia	New York, N.L.	4-1
1906	Chicago	Chicago	Chicago, A.L.	4-2
1907	Chicago	Detroit	Chicago, N.L.	4-0
1908	Chicago	Detroit	Chicago, N.L.	4-1
1909	Pittsburgh	Detroit	Pittsburgh, N.L.	4-3
1910	Chicago	Philadelphia	Philadelphia, A.L.	4-1
1911	New York	Philadelphia	Philadelphia, A.L.	4-2

YEAR	NATIONAL LEAGUE	AMERICAN LEAGUE	WORLD SERIES WINNER	SCORE
1912	New York	Boston	Boston, A.L.	4-3
1913	New York	Philadelphia	Philadelphia, A.L.	4-1
1914	Boston	Philadelphia	Boston, N.L.	4-0
1915	Philadelphia	Boston	Boston, A.L.	4-1
1916	Brooklyn	Boston	Boston, A.L.	4-1
1917	New York	Chicago	Chicago, A.L.	4-2
1918	Chicago	Boston	Boston, A.L.	4-2
1919	Cincinnati	Chicago	Cincinnati, N.L.	*5-3
1920	Brooklyn	Cleveland	Cleveland, A.L.	*5-2
1921	New York	New York	New York, N.L.	*5-3
1922	New York	New York	New York, N.L.	4-0
1923	New York	New York	New York, A.L.	4-2
1924	New York	Washington	Washington, A.L.	4-3
1925	Pittsburgh	Washington	Pittsburgh, N.L.	4-3
1926	St. Louis	New York	St. Louis, N.L.	4-3
1927	Pittsburgh	New York	New York, A.L.	4-0
1928	St. Louis	New York	New York, A.L.	4-0
1929	Chicago	Philadelphia	Philadelphia, A.L.	4-1
1930	St. Louis	Philadelphia	Philadelphia, A.L.	4-2
1931	St. Louis	Philadelphia	St. Louis, N.L.	4-3
1932	Chicago	New York	New York, A.L.	4-0
1933	New York	Washington	New York, N.L.	4-1
1934	St. Louis	Detroit	St. Louis, N.L.	4-3
1935	Chicago	Detroit	Detroit, A.L.	4-2
1936	New York	New York	New York, A.L.	4-2
1937	New York	New York	New York, A.L.	4-1
1938	Chicago	New York	New York, A.L.	4-0
1939	Cincinnati	New York	New York, A.L.	4-0
1940	Cincinnati	Detroit	Cincinnati, N.L.	4-3
1941	Brooklyn	New York	New York, A.L.	4-1
1942	St. Louis	New York	St. Louis, N.L.	4-1
1943	St. Louis	New York	New York, A.L.	4-1
1944	St. Louis	St. Louis	St. Louis, N.L.	4-2

*A nine-game World Series was played.

YEAR	NATIONAL LEAGUE	AMERICAN LEAGUE	WORLD SERIES WINNER	SCORE
1945	Chicago	Detroit	Detroit, A.L.	4-3
1946	St. Louis	Boston	St. Louis, N.L.	4-3
1947	Brooklyn	New York	New York, A.L.	4-3
1948	Boston	Cleveland	Cleveland, A.L.	4-2
1949	Brooklyn	New York	New York, A.L.	4-1
1950	Philadelphia	New York	New York, A.L.	4-0
1951	New York	New York	New York, A.L.	4-2
1952	Brooklyn	New York	New York, A.L.	4-3
1953	Brooklyn	New York	New York, A.L.	4-2
1954	New York	Cleveland	New York, N.L.	4-0
1955	Brooklyn	New York	Brooklyn, N.L.	4-3
1956	Brooklyn	New York	New York, A.L.	4-3
1957	Milwaukee	New York	Milwaukee, N.L.	4-3
1958	Milwaukee	New York	New York, A.L.	4-3
1959	Los Angeles	Chicago	Los Angeles, N.L.	4-2
1960	Pittsburgh	New York	Pittsburgh, N.L.	4-3
1961	Cincinnati	New York	New York, A.L.	4-1
1962	San Francisco	New York	New York, A.L.	4-3
1963	Los Angeles	New York	Los Angeles, N.L.	4-0
1964	St. Louis	New York	St. Louis, N.L.	4-3
1965	Los Angeles	Minnesota	Los Angeles, N.L.	4-3
1966	Los Angeles	Baltimore	Baltimore, A.L.	4-0
1967	St. Louis	Boston	St. Louis, N.L.	4-3
1968	St. Louis	Detroit	Detroit, A.L.	4-3
1969	New York	Baltimore	New York, N.L.	4-1
1970	Cincinnati	Baltimore	Baltimore, A.L.	4-1
1971	Pittsburgh	Baltimore	Pittsburgh, N.L.	4-3
1972	Cincinnati	Oakland	Oakland, A.L.	4-3
1973	New York	Oakland	Oakland, A.L.	4-3
1974	Los Angeles	Oakland	Oakland, A.L.	4-1
1975	Cincinnati	Boston	Cincinnati, N.L.	4-3
1976	Cincinnati	New York	Cincinnati, N.L.	4-0
1977	Los Angeles	New York	New York, A.L.	4-2
1978	Los Angeles	New York	New York, A.L.	4-2

THE ALL-STAR GAMES

Highlights of Interleague Competition

The brainstorm of Chicago newspaperman Arch Ward, the All-Star Game began as an exhibition to promote the Chicago World's Fair.

Since the first game in 1933, which was highlighted by a Babe Ruth homer, 49 games have been played. The National League has won 30 games; the American League has won 18. The 1961 game ended in a 1-1 tie, called on account of rain.

Date	Place	Winners	Score	Attendance
July 6, 1933	Chicago (A.L.)	Americans	4-2	47,595
July 10, 1934	New York (N.L.)	Americans	9-7	48,363
July 8, 1935	Cleveland (A.L.)	Americans	4-1	69,831
July 7, 1936	Boston (N.L.)	Nationals	4-3	25,556
July 7, 1937	Washington (A.L.)	Americans	8-3	31,391
July 6, 1938	Cincinnati (N.L.)	Nationals	4-1	27,067
July 11, 1939	New York (A.L.)	Americans	3-1	62,892
July 9, 1940	St. Louis (N.L.)	Nationals	4-0	32,373
July 8, 1941	Detroit (A.L.)	Americans	7-5	54,674
July 6, 1942	New York (N.L.)	Americans	3-1	34,178
July 13, 1943	Philadelphia (A.L.)	Americans	5-3	31,938
July 11, 1944	Pittsburgh (N.L.)	Nationals	7-1	29,589
No game in 1945				
July 9, 1946	Boston (A.L.)	Americans	12-0	34,906
July 8, 1947	Chicago (N.L.)	Americans	2-1	41,123
July 12, 1948	St. Louis (A.L.)	Americans	5-2	34,009

July 12, 1949	Brooklyn (N.L.)	Americans	11-7	32,577
July 11, 1950	Chicago (A.L.)	Nationals	4-3	46,127
July 10, 1951	Detroit (A.L.)	Nationals	8-3	52,075
July 8, 1952	Philadelphia (N.L.)	Nationals	3-2	32,785
July 14, 1953	Cincinnati (N.L.)	Nationals	5-1	30,846
July 13, 1954	Cleveland (A.L.)	Americans	11-9	68,751
July 12, 1955	Milwaukee (N.L.)	Nationals	6-5	45,643
July 10, 1956	Washington (A.L.)	Nationals	7-3	28,843
July 9, 1957	St. Louis (N.L.)	Americans	6-5	30,693
July 8, 1958	Baltimore (A.L.)	Americans	4-3	48,829
July 7, 1959	Pittsburgh (N.L.)	Nationals	5-4	35,277
Aug. 3, 1959	Los Angeles (N.L.)	Americans	5-3	54,982
July 11, 1960	Kansas City (A.L.)	Nationals	5-3	30,619
July 13, 1960	New York (A.L.)	Nationals	6-0	38,362
July 11, 1961	San Francisco (N.L.)	Nationals	5-4	44,115
July 31, 1961	Boston (A.L.)	Tie	1-1	31,851
July 10, 1962	Washington (A.L.)	Nationals	3-1	45,480
July 30, 1962	Chicago (N.L.)	Americans	9-4	38,359
July 9, 1963	Cleveland (A.L.)	Nationals	5-3	44,160
July 7, 1964	New York (N.L.)	Nationals	7-4	50,844
July 13, 1965	Bloomington (A.L.)	Nationals	6-5	46,706
July 12, 1966	St. Louis (N.L.)	Nationals	2-1	49,936
July 11, 1967	Anaheim (A.L.)	Nationals	2-1	46,309
July 9, 1968	Houston (N.L.)	Nationals	1-0	48,321
July 23, 1969	Washington (A.L.)	Nationals	9-3	45,259
July 14, 1970	Cincinnati (N.L.)	Nationals	5-4	51,838
July 13, 1971	Detroit (A.L.)	Americans	6-4	53,559
July 25, 1972	Atlanta (N.L.)	Nationals	4-3	53,107
July 24, 1973	Kansas City (A.L.)	Nationals	7-1	40,849
July 23, 1974	Pittsburgh (N.L.)	Nationals	7-2	50,706
July 15, 1975	Milwaukee (A.L.)	Nationals	6-3	51,480
July 13, 1976	Philadelphia (N.L.)	Nationals	7-1	63,974
July 19, 1977	New York (A.L.)	Nationals	7-5	56,683
July 11, 1978	San Diego (N.L.)	Nationals	7-3	51,549

(N.L.)—National League Ball Park   (A.L.)—American League Ball Park

TY COBB, BABE RUTH, TRIS SPEAKER

PAUL DEAN, LLOYD WANER, PAUL WANER, DIZZY DEAN

THE HALL OF FAME

Records of baseball's immortals.

Every year, on a summer day, in the sleepy upstate village of Cooperstown, New York, they turn back the clock to a more peaceful era. Baseball, as it was played a hundred years ago, is repeated in the sights and sounds of Hall of Fame installation day, and the game at Doubleday Field.

It all began on June 12, 1939 with the installation of five greats—Babe Ruth, Ty Cobb, Christy Mathewson, Walter Johnson, and Honus Wagner. The ceremonies have continued for 40 years. There are now 167 baseball greats enshrined in the Hall of Fame, including 131 players. The rest are front-office figures.

BATTERS

NAME	SELECTED	YEARS	GAMES	AT BATS	RUNS	HITS	PCT.
*Anson, Adrian	(1939)	1876-1897	2253	9084	1712	3081	.339
Appling, Lucius	(1964)	1930-1950	2422	8857	1319	2749	.310
*Averill, H. Earl	(1975)	1929-1941	1669	6359	1224	2020	.318

*Special Committee Nominee

NAME	SELECTED	YEARS	GAMES	AT BATS	RUNS	HITS	PCT.
*Baker, J. Frank	(1955)	1908-1922	1575	5985	887	1838	.307
*Bancroft, David	(1971)	1915-1930	1913	7182	1048	2004	.279
Banks, Ernest	(1977)	1953-1971	2528	9421	1305	2583	.274
*Beckley, Jacob	(1971)	1888-1907	2373	9476	1601	2930	.309
Berra, Lawrence	(1971)	1946-1965	2120	7555	1175	2150	.285
*Bottomley, James	(1974)	1922-1937	1991	7471	1177	2313	.310
Boudreau, Louis	(1970)	1938-1952	1646	6030	861	1779	.295
*Bresnahan, Roger	(1945)	1897-1915	1410	4480	684	1251	.279
*Brouthers, Dennis	(1945)	1879-1896	1655	6737	1507	2347	.348
*Burkett, Jesse	(1946)	1890-1905	2063	8389	1708	2872	.342
Campanella, Roy	(1969)	1948-1957	1215	4205	627	1161	.276
*Carey, Max	(1961)	1910-1929	2469	9363	1545	2665	.285
*Chance, Frank	(1946)	1898-1914	1232	4279	796	1273	.297
*Clarke, Fred	(1945)	1894-1915	2204	8584	1620	2703	.315
Clemente, Roberto	(1973)	1955-1972	2433	9454	1416	3000	.317
Cobb, Tyrus	(1936)	1905-1928	3033	11429	2244	4191	.367
Cochrane, Gordon	(1947)	1925-1937	1482	5169	1041	1652	.320
Collins, Edward	(1939)	1906-1930	2826	9952	1818	3313	.333
*Collins, James	(1945)	1895-1908	1718	6792	1057	1999	.294
*Comiskey, Charles	(1939)	1882-1894	1383	5813	984	1564	.269
*Combs, Earle	(1970)	1924-1935	1454	5748	1186	1866	.325
*Connor, Roger	(1976)	1880-1897	1987	7807	1607	2535	.325
*Crawford, Samuel	(1957)	1899-1917	2505	9579	1392	2964	.309
Cronin, Joseph	(1956)	1926-1945	2124	7577	1233	2285	.302
*Cuyler, Hazen	(1968)	1921-1938	1879	7161	1305	2299	.321
*Delahanty, Edward	(1945)	1888-1903	1825	7493	1596	2593	.346
Dickey, William	(1954)	1928-1946	1789	6300	930	1969	.313
DiMaggio, Joseph	(1955)	1936-1951	1736	6821	1390	2214	.325
*Duffy, Hugh	(1945)	1888-1906	1722	6999	1545	2307	.330
*Evers, John	(1946)	1902-1919	1776	6136	919	1569	.270
*Ewing, William	(1946)	1880-1897	1280	5348	1119	1663	.311
*Flick, Elmer	(1963)	1898-1910	1480	5597	948	1764	.315
Foxx, James	(1951)	1925-1945	2317	8134	1751	2646	.325

*Special Committee Nominee

NAME	SELECTED	YEARS	GAMES	AT BATS	RUNS	HITS	PCT.
Frisch, Frank	(1947)	1919-1937	2311	9112	1532	2880	.316
Gehrig, H. Louis	(1939)	1923-1939	2164	8001	1888	2721	.340
Gehringer, Charles	(1949)	1924-1942	2323	8860	1774	2839	.320
*Goslin, Leon	(1968)	1921-1938	2287	8654	1483	2735	.316
Greenberg, Henry	(1956)	1933-1947	1394	5193	1051	1628	.313
*Hafey, Charles	(1971)	1924-1937	1283	4625	777	1466	.317
*Hamilton, William	(1961)	1888-1901	1578	6262	1694	2157	.344
Hartnett, Charles	(1955)	1922-1941	1990	6432	867	1912	.297
Heilmann, Harry	(1952)	1914-1932	2146	7787	1291	2660	.342
*Herman, William	(1975)	1931-1947	1922	7707	1163	2345	.304
*Hooper, Harry	(1971)	1909-1925	2308	8784	1429	2466	.281
Hornsby, Rogers	(1942)	1915-1937	2259	8173	1579	2930	.358
*Jennings, Hugh	(1945)	1891-1918	1264	4840	969	1520	.314
Keeler, William	(1939)	1892-1910	2124	8564	1720	2955	.345
*Kelley, Joseph	(1971)	1891-1908	1829	6989	1425	2245	.321
*Kelly, George	(1973)	1915-1932	1622	5993	819	1778	.297
*Kelly, Michael	(1945)	1878-1893	1493	6178	1434	1944	.315
Kiner, Ralph	(1975)	1946-1955	1472	5205	971	1451	.279
Lajoie, Napoleon	(1937)	1896-1916	2475	9589	1503	3251	.339
*Lindstrom, Frederick	(1976)	1924-1936	1438	5611	895	1747	.311
Mantle, Mickey	(1974)	1951-1968	2401	8102	1677	2415	.298
*Manush, Henry	(1964)	1923-1939	2009	7653	1287	2524	.330
Maranville, Walter	(1954)	1912-1935	2670	10078	1255	2605	.258
Mathews, Edwin	(1978)	1952-1968	2391	8537	1509	2315	.271
*McCarthy, Thomas	(1946)	1884-1896	1268	5098	1062	1498	.294
*McGraw, John	(1937)	1891-1906	1082	3919	1019	1307	.334
Medwick, Joseph	(1968)	1932-1948	1984	7635	1198	2471	.324
Musial, Stanley	(1969)	1941-1963	3026	10972	1949	3630	.331
*O'Rourke, James	(1945)	1876-1894	1750	7335	1425	2314	.315
Ott, Melvin	(1951)	1926-1947	2730	9456	1859	2876	.304
*Rice, Edgar	(1963)	1915-1934	2404	9269	1515	2987	.322

*Special Committee Nominee

BATTERS

NAME	SELECTED	YEARS	GAMES	AT BATS	RUNS	HITS	PCT.
Robinson, Jack	(1962)	1947-1956	1382	4877	947	1518	.311
*Robinson, Wilbert	(1945)	1886-1902	1316	4942	629	1386	.280
*Roush, Edd	(1962)	1913-1931	1967	7361	1097	2377	.323
Ruth, George	(1936)	1914-1935	2503	8399	2174	2873	.342
*Schalk, Raymond	(1955)	1912-1929	1760	5306	579	1345	.253
*Sewell, Joseph	(1977)	1920-1933	1903	7132	1141	2226	.312
Simmons, Al	(1953)	1924-1944	2215	8761	1507	2927	.334
Sisler, George	(1939)	1915-1930	2055	8267	1284	2812	.340
Speaker, Tristram	(1937)	1907-1928	2789	10208	1881	3515	.344
Terry, William	(1954)	1923-1936	1721	6428	1120	2193	.341
*Thompson, Samuel	(1974)	1885-1906	1405	6004	1259	2016	.336
*Tinker, Joseph	(1946)	1902-1916	1798	6446	770	1698	.264
Traynor, Harold	(1948)	1920-1937	1941	7559	1183	2416	.320
Wagner, John	(1936)	1897-1917	2785	10427	1740	3430	.329
*Wallace, Roderick	(1953)	1894-1918	2369	8629	1056	2308	.267
*Waner, Lloyd	(1967)	1927-1945	1993	7772	1201	2459	.316
Waner, Paul	(1952)	1926-1945	2549	9459	1626	3152	.333
*Ward, John	(1964)	1878-1894	1810	7598	1402	2151	.283
*Wheat, Zachariah	(1959)	1909-1927	2406	9106	1289	2884	.317
Williams, Theodore	(1966)	1939-1960	2292	7706	1798	2654	.344
*Youngs, Ross	(1972)	1917-1926	1211	4627	812	1491	.322

PITCHERS

NAME	SELECTED	YEARS	GAMES	IP	WINS	LOSSES	PCT.
Alexander, Grover	(1938)	1911-1930	696	5189	373	208	.642
*Bender, Charles	(1953)	1903-1925	452	3026	212	128	.624
*Brown, Mordecai	(1949)	1903-1916	480	3168	239	130	.648
*Chesbro, John	(1946)	1899-1909	384	2859	199	128	.609
*Clarkson, John	(1963)	1882-1894	529	4514	328	175	.652
*Coveleski, Stanley	(1969)	1912-1928	449	3092	216	142	.603
Dean, Jerome	(1953)	1930-1947	317	1966	150	83	.644

*Special Committee Nominee

PITCHERS

NAME	SELECTED	YEARS	GAMES	IP	WINS	LOSSES	PCT.
*Faber, Urban	(1964)	1914-1933	669	4087	253	211	.545
Feller, Robert	(1962)	1936-1956	570	3828	266	162	.621
Ford, Edward	(1974)	1950-1967	498	3171	236	106	.690
*Galvin, James	(1965)	1876-1892	680	5959	365	309	.542
*Gomez, Vernon	(1972)	1930-1943	368	2503	189	102	.649
*Griffith, Clark	(1946)	1891-1914	428	3370	237	140	.629
*Grimes, Burleigh	(1964)	1916-1934	615	4178	270	212	.560
Grove, Robert	(1947)	1925-1941	616	3940	300	141	.680
*Haines, Jesse	(1970)	1918-1937	555	3207	210	158	.571
*Hoyt, Waite	(1969)	1918-1938	675	3762	237	182	.566
Hubbell, Carl	(1947)	1928-1943	535	3591	253	154	.622
Johnson, Walter	(1936)	1907-1927	802	5924	416	279	.599
*Joss, Adrian	(1978)	1902-1910	284	2342	159	96	.625
*Keefe, Timothy	(1964)	1880-1893	577	5039	346	225	.606
Koufax, Sanford	(1971)	1955-1966	397	2325	165	87	.655
Lemon, Robert	(1976)	1946-1958	460	2849	207	128	.618
Lyons, Theodore	(1955)	1923-1946	594	4162	260	230	.531
*Marquard, Richard	(1971)	1908-1925	537	3307	201	177	.532
Mathewson, Christopher	(1936)	1900-1916	634	4789	373	188	.665
*McGinnity, Joseph	(1946)	1899-1908	467	3455	247	142	.633
*Nichols, Charles	(1949)	1890-1906	582	5015	360	202	.641
Pennock, Herbert	(1948)	1912-1934	617	3559	241	163	.597
*Plank, Edward	(1946)	1901-1917	620	4503	325	190	.631
*Radbourne, Charles	(1939)	1880-1891	517	4543	308	191	.617
*Rixey, Eppa	(1963)	1912-1933	692	4494	266	251	.515
Roberts, Robin	(1976)	1948-1966	676	4689	286	245	.539
Ruffing, Charles	(1967)	1924-1947	624	4342	273	225	.548
*Rusie, Amos	(1977)	1889-1901	412	3770	247	174	.587
Ruth, George	(1936)	1914-1933	163	1220	92	44	.676
Spahn, Warren	(1973)	1942-1965	750	5246	363	245	.597

*Special Committee Nominee

PITCHERS

NAME	SELECTED	YEARS	GAMES	IP	WINS	LOSSES	PCT.
Vance, Arthur	(1955)	1915-1935	442	2967	197	140	.585
*Waddell, George	(1946)	1897-1910	407	2958	193	140	.580
*Walsh, Edward	(1946)	1904-1917	431	2968	195	126	.607
*Welch, Michael	(1973)	1880-1892	564	4774	311	207	.600
Wynn, Early	(1972)	1939-1963	691	4566	300	244	.551
Young, Denton	(1937)	1890-1911	906	7377	511	315	.619

SELECTED FOR MERITORIOUS SERVICE

EDWARD BARROW	Manager-Executive
JAMES BELL	Negro League Player
MORGAN G. BULKELEY	Executive
ALEXANDER J. CARTWRIGHT	Executive
HENRY CHADWICK	Writer-Statistician
OSCAR CHARLESTON	Negro League Player
JOHN CONLAN	Umpire
THOMAS CONNOLLY	Umpire
WILLIAM A. CUMMINGS	Early Pitcher
MARTIN DIHIGO	Negro League Player
WILLIAM G. EVANS	Umpire-Executive
FORD C. FRICK	Commissioner-Executive
JOSH GIBSON	Negro League Player
WILLIAM HARRIDGE	Executive
STANLEY R. HARRIS	Player-Manager
R. CALVIN HUBBARD	Umpire
MILLER J. HUGGINS	Manager
MONFORD M. IRVIN	Negro League Player
B. BANCROFT JOHNSON	Executive
WILLIAM JOHNSON	Negro League Player
WILLIAM KLEM	Umpire
KENESAW M. LANDIS	Commissioner
WALTER LEONARD	Negro League Player
JOHN HENRY LLOYD	Negro League Player
ALFONSO R. LOPEZ	Player-Manager
CONNIE MACK	Manager-Executive
LELAND S. MACPHAIL	Executive
JOSEPH McCARTHY	Manager
WILLIAM B. McKECHNIE	Manager
LEROY R. PAIGE	Negro League Pitcher
W. BRANCH RICKEY	Manager-Executive
ALBERT G. SPALDING	Early Player
CHARLES D. STENGEL	Player-Manager
GEORGE M. WEISS	Executive
GEORGE WRIGHT	Early Player
HARRY WRIGHT	Manager

*Special Committee Nominee

OLD TIMERS' DAY—JULY 29, 1961
ZACH WHEAT, MAX CAREY, RUBE MORGUARD

BASEBALL EXECUTIVES—1960
WARREN GILES, JOE CRONIN, CHARLES SEGAR, FORD FRICK

HOW THEY FINISHED IN '78

The 1978 season saw the New York Yankees climax one of the greatest comebacks in baseball history. They beat the Boston Red Sox 5-4 in the second playoff ever in the league to capture the AL Eastern Title.

The only other playoff occurred in 1948, when Boston lost to Cleveland.

On the morning of July 19, the Yankees trailed by 14 games.

Kansas City was an easy winner in the AL West.

Philadelphia hung on after a furious Pittsburgh finish to win the NL East for the third straight year.

The Los Angeles Dodgers, with a strong finish, won the NL West.

AMERICAN LEAGUE

WEST	W	L	PCT.	GB	EAST	W	L	PCT.	GB
Kansas City	92	70	.568	—	New York	100	63	.613	—
Texas	87	75	.537	5	Boston	99	64	.607	1
California	87	75	.537	5	Milwaukee	93	69	.574	6
Minnesota	73	89	.451	19	Baltimore	90	71	.559	8½
Chicago	71	90	.441	20½	Detroit	86	76	.531	13
Oakland	69	93	.426	23	Cleveland	69	90	.434	28½
Seattle	56	104	.350	35	Toronto	59	102	.366	39½

NATIONAL LEAGUE

WEST	W	L	PCT.	GB	EAST	W	L	PCT.	GB
Los Angeles	95	67	.586	—	Philadelphia	90	72	.556	—
Cincinnati	92	69	.571	2½	Pittsburgh	88	73	.547	1½
San Francisco	89	73	.549	6	Chicago	79	83	.488	11
San Diego	84	78	.519	11	Montreal	76	86	.469	14
Houston	74	88	.457	21	St. Louis	69	93	.426	21
Atlanta	69	93	.426	26	New York	66	96	.407	24

BASEBALL'S BEST OF 1978

HITTING

American League		National League	
Rod Carew, Minnesota	.333	Dave Parker, Pittsburgh	.334
Al Oliver, Texas	.324	Steve Garvey, Los Angeles	.316
Jim Rice, Boston	.315	Jose Cruz, Houston	.315
Lou Piniella, New York	.314	Gene Richards, San Diego	.311
Ben Oglivie, Milwaukee	.303	Dave Winfield, San Diego	.310
Leon Roberts, Seattle	.299	Jack Clark, San Francisco	.306
Amos Otis, Kansas City	.298	Pete Rose, Cincinnati	.302
Fred Lynn, Boston	.298	Jeff Burroughs, Atlanta	.301
Thurman Munson, New York	.297	Dave Concepcion, Cincinnati	.301
Lyman Bostock, California	.296	Enos Cabell, Houston	.295

PITCHING

American League			National League		
Ron Guidry, New York	25-3	.893	Gaylord Perry, San Diego	21-6	.778
Bob Stanley, Boston	15-2	.882	Don Robinson, Pittsburgh	14-6	.700
Larry Gura, Kansas City	16-4	.800	Bill Bonham, Chicago	11-5	.688
Dennis Eckersley, Boston	20-8	.714	Burt Hooton, Los Angeles	19-10	.655
Mike Caldwell, Milwaukee	22-9	.710	Ross Grimsley, Montreal	20-11	.645
Ferguson Jenkins, Texas	18-8	.692	Vida Blue, San Francisco	18-10	.643
Ed Figueroa, New York	20-9	.690	Doug Rau, Los Angeles	15-9	.625
Steve Comer, Texas	11-5	.688	Pat Zachry, New York	10-6	.625

HOW THEY'LL FINISH IN 1979

—by Maury Allen

My Predictions:

- California, with Nolan Ryan making a strong comeback, should be the best team in baseball.

- Texas will improve to challenge for the American League West.

- Baltimore will come up from fourth place to break the Yankee record of three straight AL East titles.

- Look for Cincinnati and Pittsburgh to be the powers in the National League with Montreal a serious challenger to the Pirates, and the Dodgers just losing out, at the end, to the Reds.

- Tom Seaver and Joe Morgan will spark the Cincinnati comeback.

THE 1979 STANDINGS

National League East

1. Pittsburgh
2. Montreal
3. St. Louis
4. Chicago
5. Philadelphia
6. New York

National League West

1. Cincinnati
2. Los Angeles
3. San Diego
4. San Francisco
5. Atlanta
6. Houston

American League East

1. Baltimore
2. New York
3. Cleveland
4. Milwaukee
5. Detroit
6. Boston
7. Toronto

American League West

1. California
2. Texas
3. Chicago
4. Kansas City
5. Minnesota
6. Seattle
7. Oakland

STARS OF TODAY

The boys whose pictures follow are the biggest guns in the game. Most of them have been chosen for baseball's All-Star Team honors during one season or another.

There are about 600 ballplayers indentured to Major League teams today. The 60 star players whose pictures appear here represent roughly the top 10 percent of today's big-time talent.

The men who stand at the head of the class hail from 26 different states, and Cuba, Panama, and the Dominican Republic. California has provided seven of these top stars.

Twenty-five of the top men are outfielders and 13 are pitchers. The oldest star is Willie McCovey of the San Francisco Giants, born in January, 1938. The youngest star, Ruppert Jones of the Seattle Mariners, was born on March 12, 1965, only 13 days after the next youngest, Lee Mazzilli of the New York Mets.

Outside of the fact that at least one player was chosen from each Major League team, selections, generally speaking, were based on the overall record of each man throughout his career rather than on his particular performance in any one season.

Some of the stalwarts on the next pages are destined to be enshrined as baseball immortals in the Cooperstown Hall of Fame. Can you prophesy whom?

PHIL GARNER

Born April 30, 1949—Jefferson City, Tennessee

Infielder, Pittsburgh Pirates

Bats Right—Throws Right

MAJOR LEAGUE TOTALS
At Bats—2,189
Hits—560
Home Runs—41
Batting Average—.256

STEVE CARLTON
Born December 22, 1944—Miami, Florida

Pitcher, Philadelphia Phillies
Bats Left—Throws Left

MAJOR LEAGUE TOTALS
Won—207   Lost—149
Strikeouts—2,372
Bases on Balls—1,211

RON LEFLORE
Born June 16, 1948—Detroit, Michigan

Outfielder, Detroit Tigers
Bats Right—Throws Right

MAJOR LEAGUE TOTALS
At Bats—2,666
Hits—790
Home Runs—42
Batting Average—.296

RUPPERT JONES
Born March 12, 1955—Dallas, Texas

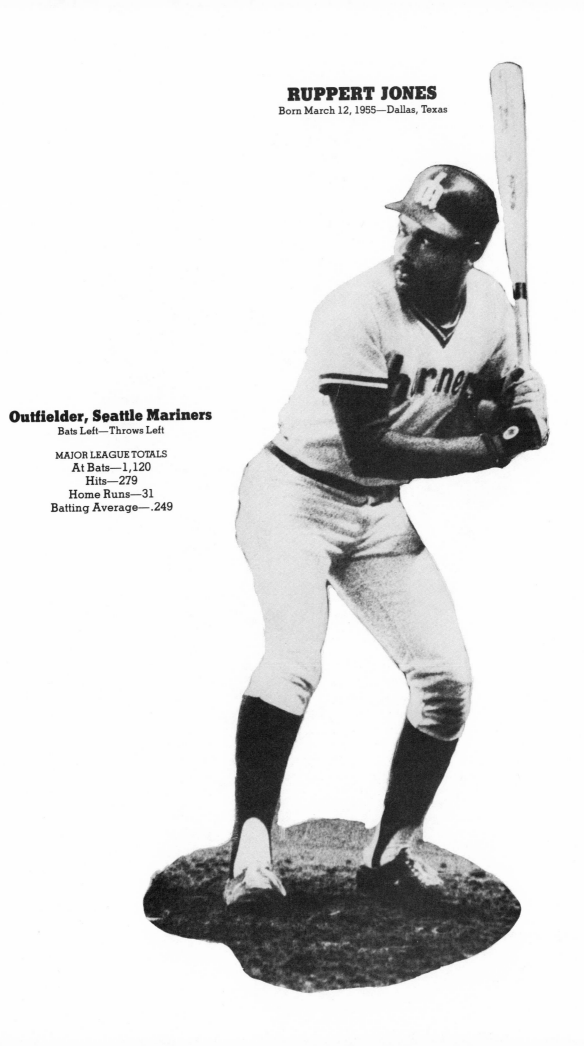

Outfielder, Seattle Mariners
Bats Left—Throws Left

MAJOR LEAGUE TOTALS
At Bats—1,120
Hits—279
Home Runs—31
Batting Average—.249

Outfielder, San Diego Padres
Bats Right—Throws Right

MAJOR LEAGUE TOTALS
At Bats—2,842
Hits—796
Home Runs—100
Batting Average—.280

DAVE WINFIELD
Born October 3, 1951—St. Paul, Minnesota

Pitcher, New York Yankees
Bats Right—Throws Right

MAJOR LEAGUE TOTALS
Won—204   Lost—148
Strikeouts—2,166
Bases on Balls—974

LUIS TIANT
Born November 23, 1940—Havana, Cuba

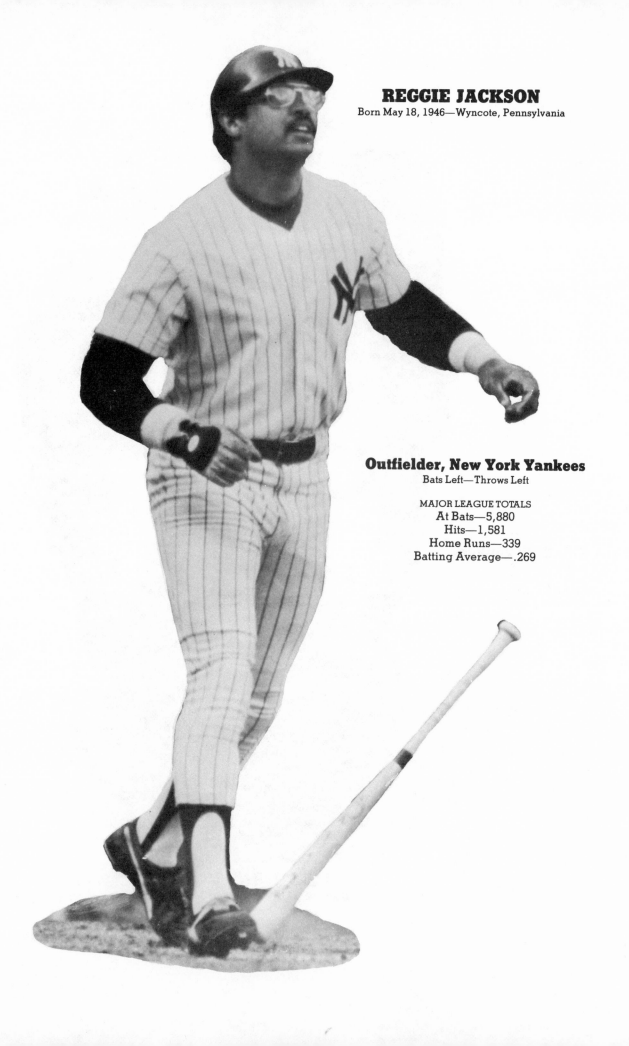

REGGIE JACKSON
Born May 18, 1946—Wyncote, Pennsylvania

Outfielder, New York Yankees
Bats Left—Throws Left

MAJOR LEAGUE TOTALS
At Bats—5,880
Hits—1,581
Home Runs—339
Batting Average—.269

ROBIN YOUNT
Born September 16, 1955—Danville, Illinois

Shortstop, Milwaukee Brewers
Bats Right—Throws Right

MAJOR LEAGUE TOTALS
At Bats—2,647
Hits—717
Home Runs—26
Batting Average—.271

VIDA BLUE

Born July 28, 1949—Mansfield, Louisiana

Pitcher, San Francisco Giants

Bats Both—Throws Left

MAJOR LEAGUE TOTALS
Won—142   Lost—96
Strikeouts—1,486
Bases on Balls—687

ROD CAREW
Born October 1, 1945—Gatun, Panama

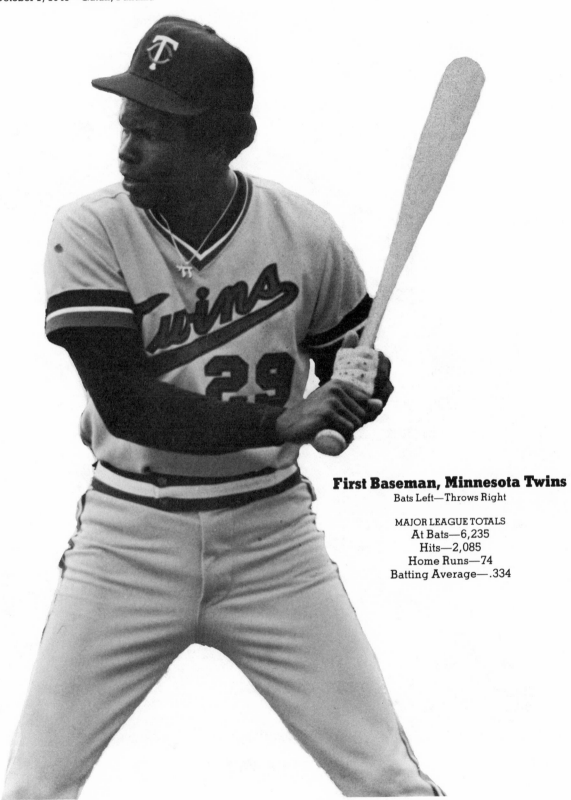

First Baseman, Minnesota Twins
Bats Left—Throws Right

MAJOR LEAGUE TOTALS
At Bats—6,235
Hits—2,085
Home Runs—74
Batting Average—.334

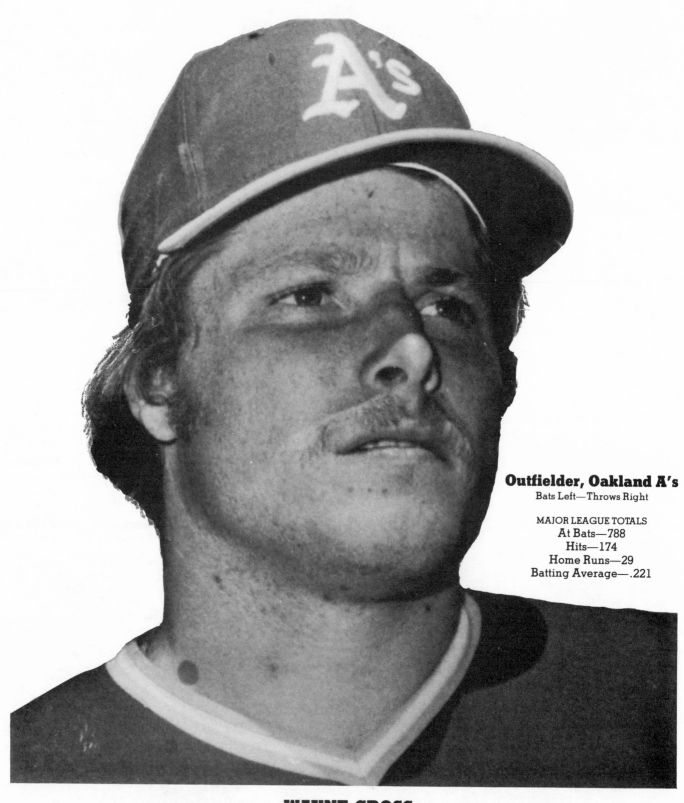

Outfielder, Oakland A's
Bats Left—Throws Right

MAJOR LEAGUE TOTALS
At Bats—788
Hits—174
Home Runs—29
Batting Average—.221

WAYNE GROSS
Born January 14, 1952—Riverside, California

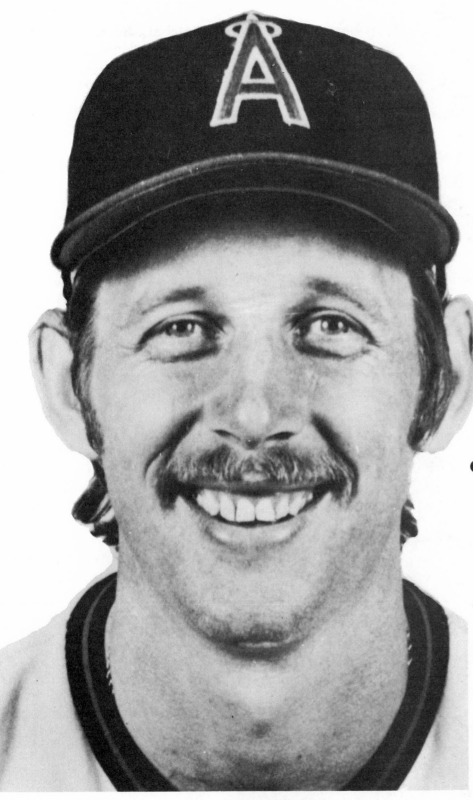

Outfielder, California Angels

Bats Right—Throws Right

MAJOR LEAGUE TOTALS
At Bats—4,539
Hits—1,237
Home Runs—141
Batting Average—.273

JOE RUDI
Born September 7, 1946—Modesto, California

Catcher, Cincinnati Reds
Bats Right—Throws Right

MAJOR LEAGUE TOTALS
At Bats—5,947
Hits—1,593
Home Runs—310
Batting Average—.268

JOHNNY BENCH
Born December 7, 1947—Oklahoma City, Oklahoma

Outfielder, Chicago Cubs
Bats Right—Throws Right

MAJOR LEAGUE TOTALS
At Bats—3,052
Hits—709
Home Runs—204
Batting Average—.232

DAVE KINGMAN
Born December 21, 1948—Pendleton, Oregon

Catcher, Texas Rangers
Bats Right—Throws Right

MAJOR LEAGUE TOTALS
At Bats—2,259
Hits—563
Home Runs—24
Batting Average—.249

JIM SUNDBERG
Born May 18, 1951—Galesburg, Illinois

Outfielder, St. Louis Cardinals

Bats Left—Throws Left

MAJOR LEAGUE TOTALS
At Bats—10,027
Hits—2,900
Home Runs—144
Batting Average—.289

LOU BROCK
Born June 18, 1939—El Dorado, Arkansas

JOHN CANDELARIA
Born November 6, 1953—Brooklyn, New York

Pitcher, Pittsburgh Pirates
Bats Left—Throws Left

MAJOR LEAGUE TOTALS
Won—56   Lost—29
Strikeouts—460
Bases on Balls—195

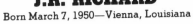

J.R. RICHARD
Born March 7, 1950—Vienna, Louisiana

Pitcher, Houston Astros

Bats Right—Throws Right

MAJOR LEAGUE TOTALS
Won—79   Lost—54
Strikeouts—1,061
Bases on Balls—632

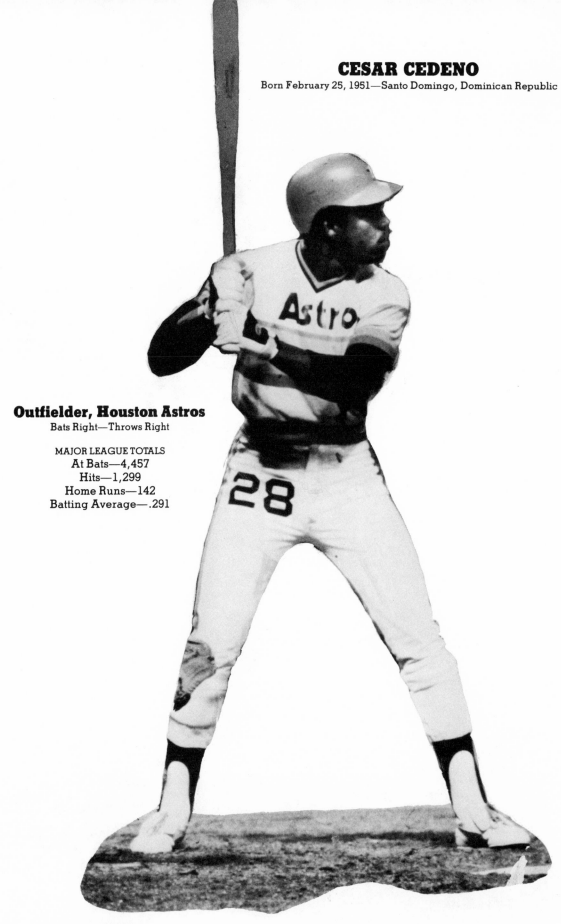

CESAR CEDENO
Born February 25, 1951—Santo Domingo, Dominican Republic

Outfielder, Houston Astros
Bats Right—Throws Right

MAJOR LEAGUE TOTALS
At Bats—4,457
Hits—1,299
Home Runs—142
Batting Average—.291

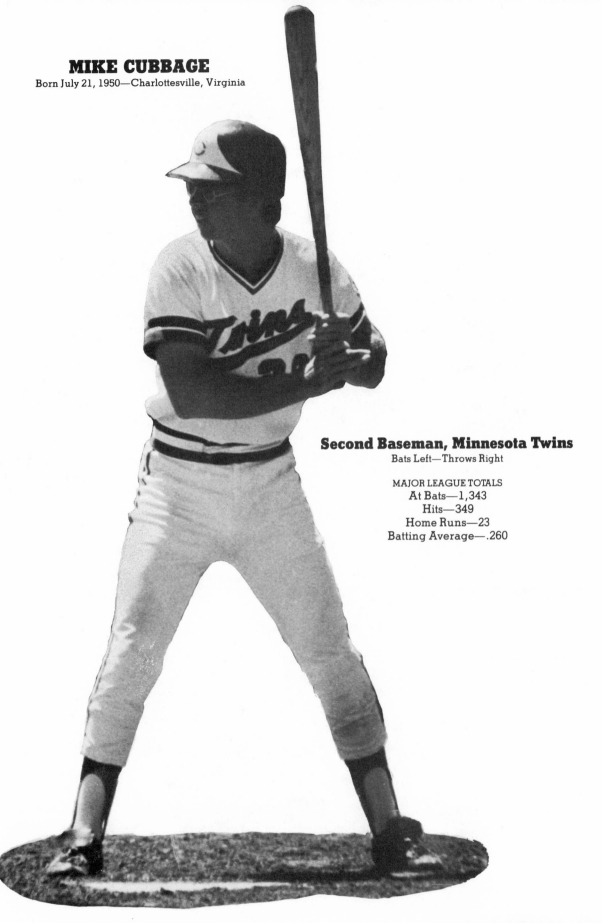

MIKE CUBBAGE
Born July 21, 1950—Charlottesville, Virginia

Second Baseman, Minnesota Twins
Bats Left—Throws Right

MAJOR LEAGUE TOTALS
At Bats—1,343
Hits—349
Home Runs—23
Batting Average—.260

Outfielder, Atlanta Braves
Bats Right—Throws Right

MAJOR LEAGUE TOTALS
At Bats—3,204
Hits—915
Home Runs—99
Batting Average—.286

GARY MATTHEWS
Born July 5, 1950—San Fernando, California

Pitcher, New York Yankees
Bats Left—Throws Left

MAJOR LEAGUE TOTALS
Won—41   Lost—11
Strikeouts—451
Bases on Balls—150

RON GUIDRY
Born August 28, 1950—Lafayette, Louisiana

JOHN MAYBERRY
Born February 18, 1950—Detroit, Michigan

First Baseman, Toronto Blue J
Bats Left—Throws Left

MAJOR LEAGUE TOTALS
At Bats—3,944
Hits—1,002
Home Runs—177
Batting Average—.254

WILLIE McCOVEY
Born January 10, 1938—Mobile, Alabama

First Baseman, San Francisco Giants
Bats Left—Throws Left

MAJOR LEAGUE TOTALS
At Bats—7,731
Hits—2,100
Home Runs—505
Batting Average—.272

Outfielder, New York Mets
Bats Both —Throws Right

MAJOR LEAGUE TOTALS
At Bats—1,156
Hits—297
Home Runs—24
Batting Average—.257

LEE MAZZILLI
Born March 25, 1955—Brooklyn, New York

Outfielder, Kansas City Royals
Bats Right—Throws Right

MAJOR LEAGUE TOTALS
At Bats—2,269
Hits—633
Home Runs—36
Batting Average—.279

AL COWENS
Born October 25, 1951—Los Angeles, California

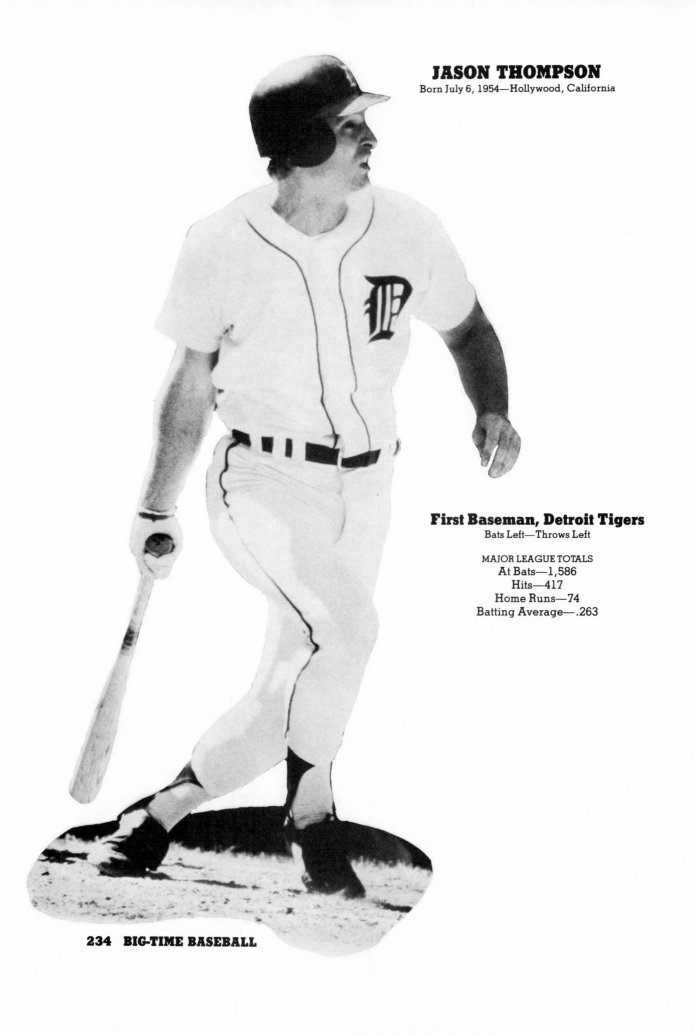

JASON THOMPSON
Born July 6, 1954—Hollywood, California

First Baseman, Detroit Tigers
Bats Left—Throws Left

MAJOR LEAGUE TOTALS
At Bats—1,586
Hits—417
Home Runs—74
Batting Average—.263

234   BIG-TIME BASEBALL

RICK CERONE

Born May 19, 1954—Newark, New Jersey

Catcher, Toronto Blue Jays

Bats Right—Throws Right

MAJOR LEAGUE TOTALS
At Balts—410
Hits—88
Home Runs—4
Batting Average—.215

Pitcher, San Diego Padres
Bats Right—Throws Left

MAJOR LEAGUE TOTALS
Won—76   Lost—80
Strikeouts—512
Bases on Balls—321

RANDY JONES
Born January 12, 1950—Fullerton, California

Second Baseman, Cleveland Indians
Bats Left—Throws Right

MAJOR LEAGUE TOTALS
At Bats—2,031
Hits—569
Home Runs—1
Batting Average—.280

DUANE KUIPER
Born June 19, 1950—Racine, Wisconsin

LARRY HISLE

Born May 5, 1947—Portsmouth, Ohio

Outfielder, Milwaukee Brewers

Bats Right—Throws Right

MAJOR LEAGUE TOTALS
At Bats—3,931
Hits—1,078
Home Runs—151
Batting Average—.274

RUSTY STAUB
Born April 1, 1944—New Orleans, Louisiana

Outfielder, Detroit Tigers
Bats Left—Throws Right

MAJOR LEAGUE TOTALS
At Bats—8,436
Hits—2,364
Home Runs—258
Batting Average—.280

MIKE SCHMIDT
Born September 27, 1949—Dayton, Ohio

Third Baseman, Philadelphia Phillies
Bats Right—Throws Right

MAJOR LEAGUE TOTALS
At Bats—3,172
Hits—800
Home Runs—190
Batting Average—.252

KEN SINGLETON

Born June 10, 1947—New York City, New York

Outfielder, Baltimore Orioles
Bats Both—Throws Right

MAJOR LEAGUE TOTALS
At Bats—4,242
Hits—1,224
Home Runs—136
Batting Average—.289

First Baseman, Chicago White Sox
Bats Left—Throws Right

MAJOR LEAGUE TOTALS
At Bats—1,333
Hits—391
Home Runs—52
Batting Average—.293

RON BLOMBERG
Born August 23, 1948—Atlanta, Georgia

Pitcher, New York Yankees
Bats Right—Throws Right

MAJOR LEAGUE TOTALS
Won—222   Lost—157
Strikeouts—1,978
Bases on Balls—920

CATFISH HUNTER
Born April 8, 1946—Hertford, North Carolina

MARK BELANGER
Born June 8, 1944—Pittsfield, Massachusetts

Shortstop, Baltimore Orioles
Bats Right—Throws Right

MAJOR LEAGUE TOTALS
At Bats—5,129
Hits—1,187
Home Runs—19
Batting Average—.231

STEVE GARVEY
Born December 22, 1948—Tampa, Florida

First Baseman, Los Angeles Dodgers
Bats Right—Throws Right

MAJOR LEAGUE TOTALS
At Bats—4,181
Hits—1,266
Home Runs—131
Batting Average—.303

Outfielder, San Francisco Giants
Bats Right—Throws Right

MAJOR LEAGUE TOTALS
At Bats—1,124
Hits—312
Home Runs—40
Batting Average—.278

JACK CLARK
Born November 10, 1955—New Brighton, Pennsylvania

Outfielder, Chicago Cubs
Bats Left—Throws Right

MAJOR LEAGUE TOTALS
At Bats—5,699
Hits—1,594
Home Runs—210
Batting Average—.280

BOBBY MURCER
Born May 20, 1946—Oklahoma City, Oklahoma

GEORGE BRETT
Born May 15, 1953—Wheeling, West Virginia

Outfielder, Cleveland Indians
Bats Left—Throws Right

MAJOR LEAGUE TOTALS
At Bats—1,850
Hits—504
Home Runs—17
Batting Average—.272

RICK MANNING
Born September 2, 1954—Niagara Falls, New York

GREG LUZINSKI
Born November 22, 1950—Chicago, Illinois

Outfielder, Philadelphia Phillies
Bats Right—Throws Right

MAJOR LEAGUE TOTALS
At Bats—3,810
Hits—1,101
Home Runs—186
Batting Average—.289

SAL BANDO
Born February 13, 1944—Cleveland, Ohio

Third Baseman, Milwaukee Brewers
Bats Right—Throws Right

MAJOR LEAGUE TOTALS
At Bats—6,265
Hits—1,610
Home Runs—226
Batting Average—.257

Outfielder, Montreal Expos
Bats Left—Throws Left

MAJOR LEAGUE TOTALS
At Bats—1,325
Hits—375
Home Runs—15
Batting Average—.283

WARREN CROMARTIE
Born September 29, 1953—Miami Beach, Florida

Designated Hitter, Kansas City Royals
Bats Right—Throws Right

MAJOR LEAGUE TOTALS
At Bats—3,798
Hits—1,096
Home Runs—96
Batting Average—.289

HAL McRAE
Born July 10, 1946—Avon Park, Florida

DAVE PARKER
Born June 9, 1951—Jackson, Mississippi

Outfielder, Pittsburgh Pirates
Bats Left—Throws Right

MAJOR LEAGUE TOTALS
At Bats—2,671
Hits—851
Home Runs—97
Batting Average—.319

JIM PALMER
Born October 15, 1945—New York City, New York

Pitcher, Baltimore Orioles
Bats Right—Throws Right

MAJOR LEAGUE TOTALS
Won—215   Lost—116
Strikeouts—1,860
Bases on Balls—1,049

Catcher, New York Mets
Bats Right—Throws Right

MAJOR LEAGUE TOTALS
At Bats—1,182
Hits—294
Home Runs—32
Batting Average—.249

JOHN STEARNS
Born August 21, 1951—Denver, Colorado

Outfielder, New York Yankees
Bats Left—Throws Left

MAJOR LEAGUE TOTALS
At Bats—3,375
Hits—981
Home Runs—36
Batting Average—.291

MICKEY RIVERS
Born October 31, 1948—Miami, Florida

Outfielder, Boston Red Sox
Bats Left—Throws Right

MAJOR LEAGUE TOTALS
At Bats—9,930
Hits—2,869
Home Runs—383
Batting Average—.289

CARL YASTRZEMSKI
Born August 22, 1939—Southhampton, New York

Catcher, St. Louis Cardinals
Bats Both—Throws Right

MAJOR LEAGUE TOTALS
At Bats—4,782
Hits—1,427
Home Runs—125
Batting Average—.298

TED SIMMONS
Born August 9, 1949—Highland Park, Michigan

Pitcher, San Diego Padres
Bats Right—Throws Right

MAJOR LEAGUE TOTALS
Won—81   Lost—83
Strikeouts—959
Bases on Balls—358

ROLLIE FINGERS

Born August 25, 1946—Steubenville, Ohio

Pitcher, Montreal Expos
Bats Left—Throws Left

MAJOR LEAGUE TOTALS
Won—107   Lost—79
Strikeouts—661
Bases on Balls—460

ROSS GRIMSLEY
Born January 7, 1950—Topeka, Kansas

PETE ROSE
Born April, 14, 1942—Cincinnati, Ohio

Third Baseman, Cincinnati Reds
Bats Both—Throws Right

MAJOR LEAGUE TOTALS
At Bats—10,196
Hits—3,164
Home Runs—150
Batting Average—.310

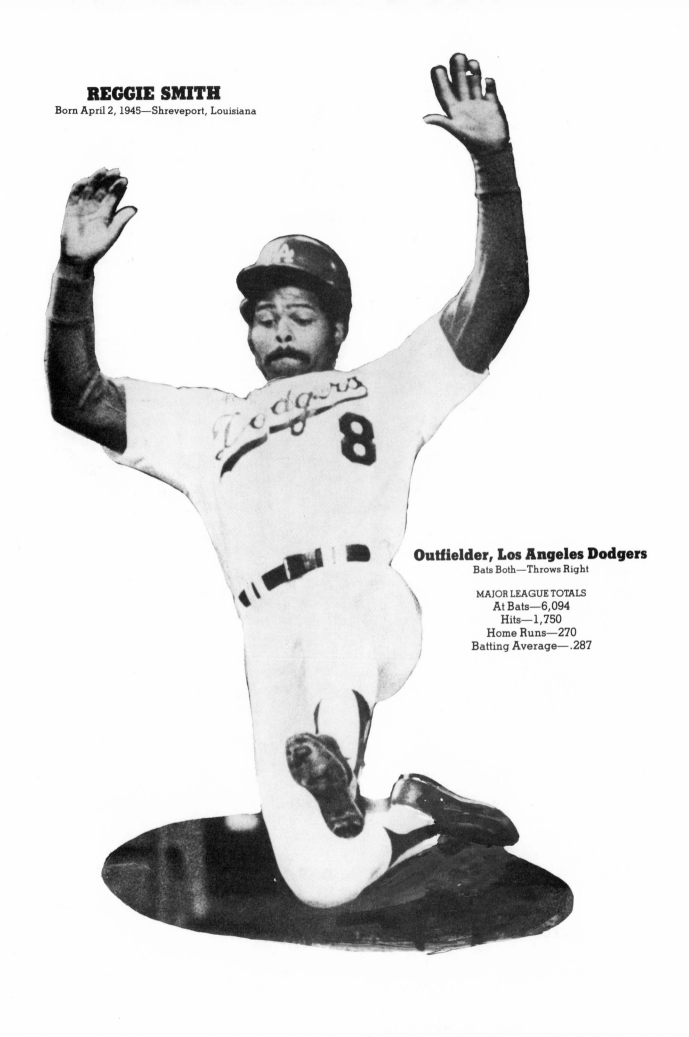

REGGIE SMITH
Born April 2, 1945—Shreveport, Louisiana

Outfielder, Los Angeles Dodgers
Bats Both—Throws Right

MAJOR LEAGUE TOTALS
At Bats—6,094
Hits—1,750
Home Runs—270
Batting Average—.287

Second Baseman, Los Angeles Dodgers

Bats Right—Throws Right

MAJOR LEAGUE TOTALS
At Bats—3,241
Hits—867
Home Runs—56
Batting Average—.268

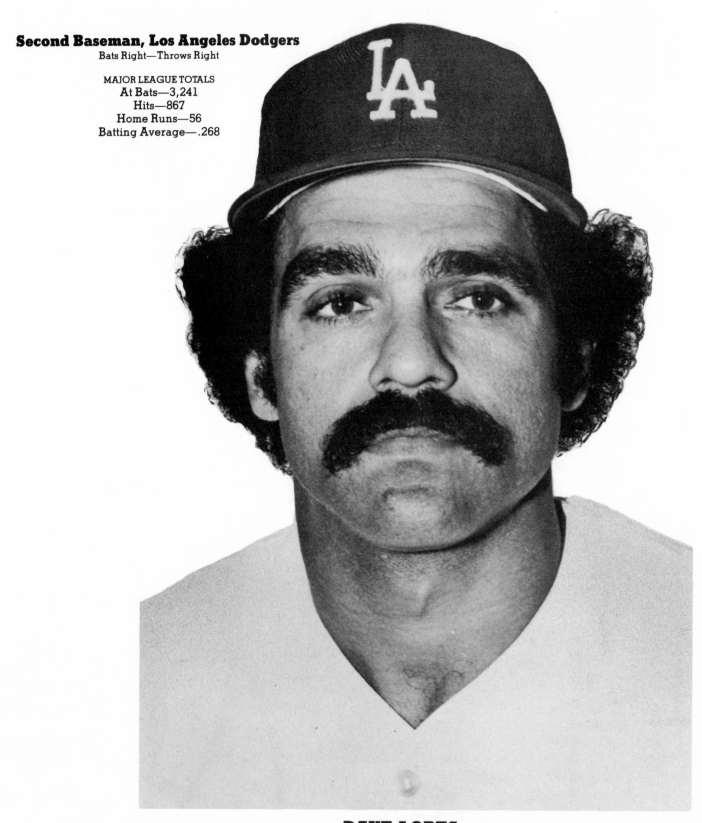

DAVE LOPES

Born May 3, 1946—East Providence, Rhode Island

Outfielder, New York Mets

Bats Right—Throws Right

MAJOR LEAGUE TOTALS
At Bats—937
Hits—260
Home Runs—22
Batting Average—.277

Bats Both—Throws Left

STEVE HENDERSON
Born November 18, 1952—Houston, Texas

Pitcher, Chicago Cubs
Bats Right—Throws Right

MAJOR LEAGUE TOTALS
Won—21   Lost—16
Strikeouts—308
Bases on Balls—83

BRUCE SUTTER
Born January 8, 1953—Lancaster, Pennsylvania

Pitcher, New York Mets

Bats Right—Throws Right

MAJOR LEAGUE TOTALS
Won—26   Lost—32
Strikeouts—318
Bases on Balls—194

CRAIG SWAN
Born November 30, 1950—Van Nuys, California

YOU'RE OUT!

A session with the rulebook.

In how many ways can a baseball player be put out? Ten? You're wrong! You double it to 20? You're still wrong! Thirty? No, even more than that!

According to the rules, there are 31 wasy in which a player can be declared out. Since we don't think that anybody except a big league ump could list all the methods of expiration, we are setting down the answers here and now.

IF YOU'RE A BATTER, YOU'RE OUT IF:

1. You fail to take your turn at the bat in accordance with the batting order.

2. You fail to take your position at the plate within one minute after the umpire has called for you.

3. You interfere with the catcher.

4. You change your position from the righthand side of the batter's box to the lefthand side or vice versa, while the pitcher is ready to pitch.

5. You hit a ball while standing outside of the batter's box.

6. You fail to get out of the way of a play made for your teammate who is stealing home.

7. You strike out.

8. You have two strikes and then you hit a foul tip which is caught.

9. You strike out and though the catcher doesn't hold the last strike, the ball has touched your body or clothing.

10. You bunt foul on the last strike.

11. You hit an infield fly with runners on first and second, or first, second, and third, and less than two out.

12. You hit a fly which is caught.

13. You bunt, and hit the ball a second time with your bat while running towards first.

14. You're thrown out at first.

IF YOU'RE A RUNNER, YOU'RE OUT IF:

15. You're tagged off base.

16. You run outside the basepaths.

17. You pass a runner on the basepaths.

18. You're hit by a batted ball.

19. You run bases in reverse order—in order to confuse the opposition—and an opposing fielder touches a ball to the base you would normally occupy.

20. After a fly is caught, you do not tag up at the base you were occupying and you're tagged with the ball on some other base.

21. You fail to avoid interfering with a fielder who is attempting to field a batted ball. The fact that you try to avoid bumping into him is immaterial.

22. You intentionally interfere with a thrown ball.

23. You deliberately knock a ball out of the mitt of the fielder who was attempting to put you out.

24. You're forced by a batted ball and a fielder holding the ball touches the bag to which you were forced.

25. You fail to touch a base and the fielder holding the ball touches the base you omitted to tag.

26. After a game is temporarily suspended, you fail to tag up on the base you occupied when time was called and you touch the next base after the pitcher delivers the ball.

27. You're on the same base occupied by a teammate.

28. Your coach physically assists you to return to base while a play is being made for you.

29. You're on third and a teammate hits an infield grounder, and your coach runs toward home in an attempt to convince the fielder the play should be made to home.

30. Your teammate who has been put out moves slowly off the basepaths and thereby obstructs a play to tag you.

31. Your teammates stand or collect around a base for which you are trying, and thereby confuse the fielder, who is making a play for you.

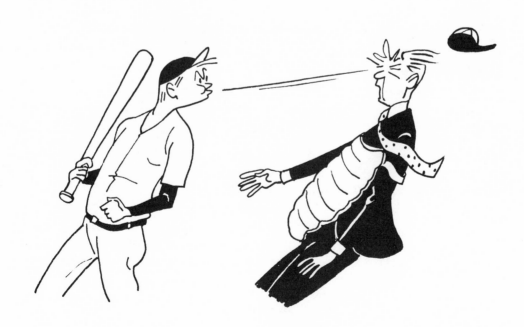

BASEBALL'S WHO'S WHO

A quiz on nicknames.

Fans of the National Pastime have endowed a great many players with special monickers. Many of these *noms de guerre* have become famous down the long history of baseball.

There are 189 nicknames in the following list of ballplayers, past, present, and mayhap forgotten. How many of these players can you identify?

A score of 100 shows you are up on your baseball. A score of 120 qualifies you as a baseball historian. A score of 140 says you are a baseball sage.

Answers on page following quiz

1. The Bambino
2. The Man of a
       Thousand Curves
3. The Iron Man
4. Arky
5. The Fordham Flash
6. The Scooter
7. Dizzy
8. The Wild Horse
       of the Osage
9. The Georgia Peach
10. Fireball
11. Antelope
12. The Big Train
13. The Flying Dutchman
14. Three-fingered Brown
15. Birdie
16. Larrupin' Lou
17. Preacher
18. Rapid Robert
19. Kiki
20. Pee Wee
21. The Rajah

22. Spider
23. Bobo
24. Old Reliable
25. The Lip
26. Wahoo Sam
27. Push-em-up Tony
28. Pie
29. The Gray Eagle
30. Little Napoleon
31. Pistol Pete
32. Harry the Horse
33. Black Mike
34. Goose
35. Big Poison
36. High Pockets
37. The Rabbit
38. Puddin' Head
39. The Whip
40. Big Six
41. King Kong
42. Peanuts
43. Schoolboy
44. Daffy

45. Mealticket
46. Stan the Man
47. Stubby
48. The Yankee Clipper
49. Jeep
50. Dazzy
51. Slatts
52. Boo
53. The Sultan of Swat
54. Old Pete
55. The Duke of Tralee
56. The Old Fox
57. Gettysburg
58. The Crab
59. Arthur the Great
60. Frenchy
61. Flash
62. Smokey Joe
63. Butch
64. Cookie
65. Irish
66. Jigger
67. Dixie

68. The Cat
69. Wee Willie
70. Big Ed
71. Happy Jack
72. Satchel
73. Turkey Mike
74. Bullet Joe
75. The Miracle Man
76. Billy the Kid
77. Goofy
78. Jumpin' Joe
79. King Carl
80. Master Melvin
81. The Peerless Leader
82. Jug Handle
83. Old Hoss
84. Country
85. Mule
86. Camera Eye
87. The Little Professor
88. Casey
89. Beauty
90. The Arkansas Traveler
91. The Old Roman
92. Memphis Bill
93. Pants
94. Ozark Ike
95. The Mad Russian
96. 'Oom Paul
97. Duster
98. Wildfire
99. Little Poison
100. Yogi
101. The Duke
102. Say Hey Kid
103. Big Klu
104. Pig
105. Jabbo
106. Dusty
107. Jungle Jim
108. Suitcase

109. The Flying Scot
110. The Thumper
111. Yoyo
112. The Barber
113. Big Bear
114. The Kitten
115. Toothpick
116. The Bull
117. Turk
118. Vinegar Bend
119. Digger
120. Pinky
121. Junior
122. Killer
123. The Switcher
124. Handy Andy
125. Twig
126. Coot
127. Skinny
128. Mudcat
129. Boom Boom
130. The Hat
131. Hondo Hurricane
132. Crabapple Comet
133. Mickey Mouse
134. Hot Potato
135. Lucky
136. Riverboat
137. Tookie
138. Specs
139. Cuddles
140. Stormy
141. Bad News
142. Boots
143. Chubby
144. General
145. Snuffy
146. Ducky
147. Sparky
148. Muddy
149. Bama

150. Grandma
151. Pancho
152. Blazer
153. Stretch
154. Bullet Bob
155. Boog
156. The Monster
157. Monbo
158. Choo-Choo
159. The Knife
160. Yaz
161. Bulldog Jim
162. Rocky
163. Ragin' Cajun
164. Big Goose
165. Sweet Lou
166. Squatty Body
167. Stick
168. Puff
169. Bucky
170. Mick the Quick
171. Iron Hands
172. The Three Million
       Dollar Man
173. Lucky Jack
174. Happy
175. Schnozz
176. The Franchise
177. The Express
178. Big D
179. Zip
180. The Count
181. Snake
182. The Hammer
183. Giggy
184. Buzz
185. Butch
186. Great
187. Pudge
188. Penguin
189. Charley Hustle

Answers to BASEBALL'S WHO'S WHO

1. Babe Ruth
2. John F. Sain
3. Joe McGinnity
4. Floyd Vaughan
5. Frank Frisch
6. Phil Rizzuto
7. Jerome Dean
8. Pepper Martin
9. Tyrus Cobb
10. Virgil Trucks
11. Emil Verban
12. Walter Johnson
13. Honus Wagner
14. Mordecai Brown
15. George Tebbetts
16. Lou Gehrig
17. Elwood Roe
18. Robert Feller
19. Hazen Cuyler
20. Harold H. Reese
21. Rogers Hornsby
22. John Jorgensen
23. Louis Newsom
24. Tommy Henrich
25. Leo Durocher
26. Sam Crawford
27. Tony Lazzeri
28. Harold Traynor
29. Tris Speaker
30. John McGraw
31. Pete Reiser
32. Harry Heilmann
33. Mickey Cochrane
34. Leon Goslin
35. Paul Waner
36. George Kelly
37. Walter Maranville
38. Willie Jones
39. Ewell Blackwell
40. Christy Mathewson
41. Charles Keller
42. Harry Lowery
43. Lynwood T. Rowe
44. Paul Dean
45. Carl Hubbell
46. Stan Musial
47. Frank Overmire
48. Joe DiMaggio

49. Lee Handley
50. Arthur Vance
51. Marty Marion
52. Dave Ferris
53. Babe Ruth
54. Grover C. Alexander
55. Roger Bresnahan
56. Clark Griffith
57. Eddie Plank
58. Johnny Evers
59. Arthur Shires
60. Stanley Bordagaray
61. Joe Gordon
62. Joe Wood
63. Walter J. Henline
64. Harry A. Lavagetto
65. Emil F. Meusel
66. Arnold J. Statz
67. Fred R. Walker
68. Harry Brecheen
69. William H. Keeler
70. Edward A. Walsh
71. John D. Chesbro
72. Leroy Paige
73. Michael J. Donlin
74. Joe Bush
75. George Stallings
76. Billy Southworth
77. Vernon Gomez
78. Joe Dugan
79. Carl Hubbell
80. Melvin Ott
81. Frank Chance
82. Johnny Morrison
83. Riggs Stephenson
84. Enos Slaughter
85. George Haas
86. Max Bishop
87. Dom DiMaggio
88. Charles Stengel
89. Dave Bancroft
90. Travis Jackson
91. Chas. A. Comiskey
92. William Terry
93. Clarence Rowland
94. Gus Zernial
95. Lou Novikoff
96. Paul Derringer

97. Walter Mails
98. Frank Schulte
99. Lloyd Waner
100. Lawrence Berra
101. Edwin D. Snider
102. Willie Mays
103. Ted Kluszewski
104. Frank House
105. Ray Jablonski
106. Jim Rhodes
107. Jim Rivera
108. Harry Simpson
109. Bobby Thomson
110. Ted Williams
111. Luis Arroyo
112. Sal Maglie
113. Mike Garcia
114. Harvey Haddix
115. Sam Jones
116. Brooks Lawrence
117. Omar Lown
118. Wilmer Mizell
119. Bill O'Dell
120. Mike Higgins
121. Jim Gilliam
122. Harmon Killebrew
123. Mickey Mantle
124. Andy Pafko
125. Wayne Terwilliger
126. Inman Veal
127. Hector Brown
128. Jim Grant
129. Walter Beck
130. Harry Walker
131. Clint Hartung
132. Johnny Rucker
133. Cliff Melton
134. Luke Hamlin
135. Jack Lohrke
136. Bob Smith
137. Harold Gilbert
138. George Toporcer
139. Clarence Marshall
140. Roy Weatherly
141. Odell Hale
142. Cletus Poffenberger
143. Lovill Dean
144. Alvin Crowder

145. George Stirnweiss
146. Joe Medwick
147. George Anderson
148. Harold Ruel
149. Carvel Rowell
150. Johnny Murphy
151. Frank Herrera
152. Don Blasingame
153. Willie McCovey
154. Bob Turley
155. John Powell
156. Dick Radatz
157. Bill Monbouquette
158. Clarence Coleman
159. Mack Jones
160. Carl Yastrzemski
161. Jim Bouton
162. Ron Swoboda
163. Ron Guidry
164. Rich Gossage
165. Lou Piniella
166. Thurman Munson
167. Gene Michael
168. Graig Nettles
169. Russell Dent
170. Mickey Rivers
171. Chuck Hiller
172. Reggie Jackson
173. Jack Lohrke
174. Burt Hooton
175. Ernie Lombardi
176. Tom Seaver
177. Nolan Ryan
178. Don Drysdale
179. Don Zimmer
180. John Montefusco
181. Pat Dobson
182. Hank Aaron
183. Al Downing
184. Lee Capra
185. Clell Hobson
186. George Scott
187. Carlton Fisk
188. Ron Cey
189. Pete Rose

SO YOU KNOW YOUR BASEBALL?

Test your knowledge of the rules.

So far as we know, no major league umpire has ever been killed in action. Yet each man jack of us, at one time or another, feels the urge to commit homicide on one of the official arbiters.

We all feel we know the game inside out. We're all quite sure we'd know *exactly* how to make the right decision in a tight spot. Well, here's a chance to stack up your knowledge of baseball against the rules book. On the following pages, you'll find 10 baseball situations. A conclusion follows each one. You're to say whether the conclusion is true or false.

The situations aren't exactly pop-ups. If you know your baseball, you ought to get at least eight right. But you're really not qualified to criticize the man in blue behind the pitcher unless you can score a clean sweep on this quiz.

You'll find the answers on the page following the quiz

1. Wild Bill O'Hara lets loose with a wild pitch. The ball strikes the ground about eight feet in front of the plate. Krinsky swats it for a home run. Wild Bill claims the ball was dead as soon as it hit the ground, and argues that the umpire should have declared the pitch a ball as soon as it struck the ground.

    The run should not be scored.

2. Ping Kane is a crossover batter; he bats lefthanded against righthanded pitchers and righthanded against southpaws. In the ninth inning of a tight game, Ping takes his place on the lefthand side of the plate. After the first pitch, he switches, taking a new stance on the righthand side of the plate. The pitcher objects, explaining that while a batter may bat lefthanded one time, and right-

handed another, he may not change his position at the plate during one lick.

The pitcher doesn't know the rules.

3. Men on first and third. Pitcher winds up, and then, in an attempt to catch the runner off first base, turns to first and throws. Umpire declares a balk. Man on first moves to second, while man on third proceeds to home. Pitcher, admitting balk, concedes that man on first may advance, but insists that man on third was not affected by play. He points out that balk was not made in play for him, and argues that runner should not be permitted to score.

The pitcher is right.

4. One out. On the pitcher's windup, the runner starts for second. He completes the steal before the ball crosses the plate. The luckless catcher not only drops the missed third strike, but pegs a wild throw to first, so that the batsman easily makes the bag. As the umpire suavely declares both runners safe, the captain of the fielding team lets out a terrific howl of protest. He demands that the batter be declared out.

The fielding captain is right.

5. Johnny X. Beanpole, a six-footer, gets up to bat. He crouches over the plate in such a way that he stands but five feet high. The pitcher puts one directly over the plate. It passes in front of Johnny's nose. If Johnny were standing up straight, the ball would have passed directly in front of his chest. The umpire calls the pitch a ball.

The umpire is in error.

6. McCarthy is on second, and Johnson's on third. On a double-steal Johnson makes for home, but the ball is whipped to the catcher in time to head him off and he seems trapped, as McCarthy stands safely on third. Somehow the fielding team can't manage to run Johnson down; and as he makes a wild dash back to third, McCarthy scrambles back to second. The umpire calls McCarthy out.

The umpire has ruled correctly.

7. Runner on second. As the batter drives a hard infield grounder to short, the runner attempts to gain third. In order not to interfere with the fielding of the ball by the shortstop, the runner properly runs behind the fielder; but just at that moment the ball takes a weird hop and the shortstop takes a wild leap backward to field the ball. He collides with the base runner. Though the runner protests that the interference was unforeseeable and that the shortstop actually bumped into *him*, the umpire declares the base runner out.

The umpire is right.

8. Casey's on first, and Lefty Gerard, the pitcher, makes as if to throw to the bag, but holds the ball. The umpire calls a balk, and then Lefty hurriedly whips the ball over the pan. The batter, Socko Hamilton, wallops it for a homer, scoring two runs. Though the fans threaten to boil him in oil, the umpire disallows both runs, orders Casey to second, and Hamilton back to the plate.

Apart from his courage, the umpire knows his baseball.

9. Two outfielders, while racing for a flyball, collide. One is so severely injured he is forced to leave the game. His team has no available substitute. When play is resumed, the two remaining outfielders move out of their usual postions so as to best cover the field. The opposing captain calls this to the attention of the umpire, objecting to the switch in playing position. The umpire, after consulting the captain of the fielding team, declares the game forfeited to the team at bat.

The umpire is right.

10. Menelli is on second and Hack Andrews is at bat. Andrews wallops a terrific drive to left field. He tears around the bases at full speed, passing Menelli between third and home. The coach waves Andrews back so that Menelli can score first. Menelli scores; but as the ball is thrown in, Andrews only has time to get back to third. The fielding pitcher tries to argue the umpire into calling Andrews out.

Andrews should be declared out.

Answers to
SO YOU KNOW YOUR BASEBALL?

1. *False.* Although it's true that a pitch which strikes the ground in front of the plate must be declared a ball even though it later passes directly over the plate, such a pitched ball is not a dead ball the moment it strikes the ground. The umpire must wait until the ball actually passes the batter before he may rule on it. If the batsman strikes at it and misses it, it is a strike, Conversely, if he hits it into fair territory, it's a hit.

2. *True.* A batter may change his position from one batting box to the other batting box as often as he wishes. The only restriction is that the batter may not so change his position while the pitcher is in the pitcher's box ready to deliver the ball.

3. *False.* When an intended throw is called a balk, all runners are entitled to advance one base.

4. *True.* A batsman is not entitled to run for first base when a third strike is dropped if first base is already occupied by a runner on his team and there are less than two out. First base is presumed to be occupied on a dropped third strike, if it was occupied by a runner at the time of the pitcher's windup. This is so even though the runner makes second before the ball crosses the plate.

5. *False.* A batter may assume any crouch at the plate he wishes, provided he is not patently attempting to make a travesty of the game. The rules require that the pitcher throw the ball over the plate, so that it passes between the batsman's knees and shoulder, *as he is standing* at the plate.

6. *False.* There is nothing in the rules that prohibits a runner who gained a base to run back to a preceding base. When a base runner occupies the base formerly held by a teammate, he doesn't necessarily force that teammate to proceed on to the next base. Both runners are privileged to recapture their former positions.

7. *True.* Intent is no consideration in fielding plays involving interference. The fielder *always* has the right of way. It is the duty of a base runner to avoid bumping into or being bumped into by a player who is fielding a ball.

8. *False.* The offensive team has an option and in this case most certainly takes the homer in preference to the balk.

9. *True.* Evidently the umpire consulted the captain to find out whether or not he had an available substitute. If a team cannot place a full contingent in the field, the game must be forfeited.

10. *True.* A batsman who passes a preceding runner is automatically out the moment he passes his teammate on the basepath.

WARREN SPAHN

CASEY AT THE BAT

The outlook wasn't brilliant for the Mudville nine that day,
The score stood two to four with just one inning left to play;
And so, when Cooney died at first, and Burrows did the same,
A sickly silence fell upon the patrons of the game.

A straggling few got up to go in deep despair. The rest
Clung to the hope that springs eternal within each human breast;
They thought if only Casey could but get a whack at that—
They'd put up *even money* now, with Casey at the bat.

But Flynn preceded Casey, and so did Jimmy Blake,
And the former was a washout, and the latter was a fake;
So upon that stricken multitude grim melancholy sat,
For there seemed but little chance of Casey's getting to the bat.

But Flynn let drive a single to the wonderment of all,
And Blake whom all had sneered at, tore the cover off the ball;
And when the dust had lifted, and they saw what had occurred,
There was Jimmy safe on second and Flynn a-huggin' third!

Then from the gladdened multitude went up a joyous yell,
It rumbled in the mountaintops, it rattled in the dell,
It struck upon the hillside and rebounded on the flat;
For Casey, mighty Casey, was advancing to the bat.

There was ease in Casey's manner as he stepped into his place,
There was pride in Casey's bearing, and a smile on Casey's face;
And when, responding to the cheers, he lightly doffed his hat,
No stranger in the crowd could doubt 'twas Casey at the bat.

Ten thousand eyes were on him as he rubbed his hands with dirt;
Five thousand tongues applauded when he wiped them on his shirt.
Then while the writhing pitcher ground the ball into his hip,
Defiance gleamed in Casey's eye, a sneer curled Casey's lip.

And now the leather-covered sphere came hurtling through the air,
And Casey stood a-watching it in haughty grandeur there;
Close by the sturdy batsman the ball unheeded sped:
"That ain't my style," said Casey. "Strike one!" the umpire said.

From the benches, black with people, there went up a muffled roar,
Like the beating of the storm-waves on a stern and distant shore;
"Kill him! Kill the umpire!" shouted someone in the stands.
And it's sure they'd have killed him had not Casey raised his hand.

With a smile of Christian charity great Casey's visage shone;
He stilled the rising tumult; he bade the game go on;
He signaled to the pitcher, and once more the spheroid flew,
But Casey still ignored it; and the umpire said, "Strike two!"

"Fraud!" cried the maddened thousands, and the echo answered "Fraud!"
But one scornful look from Casey and the audience was awed;
They saw his face grow stern and cold, they saw his muscles strain.
And they knew that Casey wouldn't let that ball go by again.

The sneer is gone from Casey's lip, his teeth are clenched with hate;
He pounds with cruel violence his bat upon the plate;
And now the pitcher holds the ball, and now he lets it go.
And now the air is shattered by the force of Casey's blow.

Oh, somewhere in this favored land the sun is shining bright;
The band is playing somewhere, and somewhere hearts are light;
And somewhere men are laughing, and somewhere children shout;
But there is no joy in Mudvelle—*mighty Casey has struck out!*

Ernest Lawrence Thayer

CASEY—20 YEARS LATER

Sequel to baseball's classic poem.

The Bugville team was surely up against a rocky game;
The chances were they'd win defeat and undying fame;
Three men were hurt and two were benched; the score stood six to four.
They had to make three hard-earned runs in just two innings more.

"It can't be done," the captain said, a pallor on his face;
"I've got two pitchers in the field, a jerk on second base;
And should another man get spiked or crippled in some way,
The team would sure be down and out, with eight men left to play.

"We're up against it anyhow as far as I can see;
My boys ain't hitting like they should and that's what worries me;
The luck is with the other side, no pennant will we win;
It's mighty tough, but we must take our medicine and grin."

The eighth round opened; one, two, three; the enemy went down;
The Bugville boys went out the same, the captain wore a frown;
The first half of the ninth came round, two men had been called out,
When Bugville's catcher broke a thumb and could not go that route.

A deathly silence settled o'er the crowd assembled there.
Defeat would be allotted them; they felt it in the air;
With only eight men in the field 'twould be a gruesome fray,—
Small wonder that the captain cursed the day he learned to play.

"Lend me a man to finish with," he begged the other team;
"Lend you a man?" the foe replied; "My boy, you're in a dream!
We want to win the pennant, too—that's what we're doing here.
There's only one thing you can do—call for a volunteer."

The captain stood and pondered in a listless sort of way;
He never was a quitter and would not be today!
"Is there within the grandstand here"—his voice rang loud and clear—
"A man who has the sporting blood to be a volunteer?"

Again that awful silence fell upon the multitude;
Was there a man among them with recklessness imbued?
The captain stood with cap in hand, while hopeless was his glance,
And then a short and stocky man cried out, "I'll take a chance."

Into the field he bounded with a step both firm and light;
"Give me the mask and mitt," he said; "let's finish up the fight.
The game is now beyond recall; I'll last at least a round;
Although I'm ancient you will find me full of pep and sound."

His hair was sprinkled here and there with little streaks of gray;
Around his eyes and on his brow a bunch of wrinkles lay.
The captain smiled despairingly and slowly turned away.
"Why, he's all right," one rooter yelled. Another, "Let him play."

"All right, go on," the captain sighed; the stranger turned around,
Took off his coat and collar, too, and threw them on the ground.
The humor of the situation seemed to hit them all,
As he donned the mask and mitt, the umpire called, "Play ball!"

Three balls the pitcher at him hurled, three balls of lightning speed;
The stranger caught them all with ease and did not seem to heed.
Each ball had been pronounced a strike, the side had been put out,
And as he walked in towards the bench, he heard the rooters shout.

One Bugville boy went out on strikes, and one was killed at first;
The captain saw his awkward pose, and gnashed his teeth and cursed.
The third man smashed a double and the fourth man swatted clear,
Then, in a thunder of applause, up came the volunteer.

His feet were planted in the earth, he swung a warlike club;
The captain saw his awkward pose and softly whispered, "Dub!"
The pitcher looked at him and grinned, then heaved a mighty ball;
The echo of that fearful swat still lingers with us all.

High, fast, and far that spheroid flew; it sailed and sailed away;
It ne'er was found, so it's supposed it still floats on today.
Three runs came in, the pennant would be Bugville's for a year;
The fans and players gathered round to cheer the volunteer.

"What is your name?" the captain asked. "Tell us your name," cried all,
As down his cheeks great tears were seen to run and then fall.
For one brief moment he was still, then murmured soft and low:
"I'm mighty Casey who struck out—just twenty years ago."

S.P. McDonald

BASEBALL'S FUNNY STORIES

It was a close and important baseball game.

Any disinterested spectator would instantly have decided that an umpire's life is not a happy one. But there were no disinterested spectators present. They were all rabid rooters and razzed the umpire unmercifully on every decision that went against the home team.

But the unrufffled ump continued to call them as he saw them. In the ninth inning, there was a close one against the home team that set the stands in an uproar.

One wrathful woman vaulted the grandstand rail and with blood in her eye, charged on the ump. Restrained from physical assault on that unhappy official by two patrolmen, she shook her fist at him and shouted, "If you were my husband, I'd give you poison!"

"Madam," the umpire replied politely, "if I were your husband, I'd take it."

The man took his wife to see a double-header. In the second inning of the second game, she rose. "Let's go, William," she said. "Isn't this where we came in?"

During spring training, the team's batting had been horribly weak. Day after day the manager sat on the bench and fumed as his charges bounced piddling grounders into the infield, and popped easy flies that would have gone for outs in the Kindergarten League.

During one practice, the manager could stand no more. In his wrath, he leaped from the dugout and grabbed the club from the batter.

"Give a look here, you guys. I'll show you," he snapped. He ordered the pitcher to toss in a few, putting everything he had on the ball.

The manager took a dozen cuts at the apple—and churned the breeze every time! After the twelfth wild miss, he threw down his bat and turned to the bench.

"That'll show you what you palookas are doing," he shouted. "Now get in there and hit."

The man had been waiting outside the ball park for an hour. When his date finally showed up, he was so angry he could hardly speak. Silently he bought the tickets and they went in. When they reached their seats it was the end of the sixth inning.

"What's the score?" she asked.

"Nothing to nothing," he answered sullenly.

"There, you see," she said triumphantly, "we haven't missed a thing!"

A small social club was in the process of getting up a baseball team. Eight players they could muster, but they were hard put to find a ninth. In desperation, they called on a new member, an Englishman, to join the team.

In their first game, the Englishman came to bat. On the first pitch, he swung and connected. Then he stood and watched while the ball soared over the fence and out of the park.

"Run!" his teammates cried. "For Pete's sake, run!"

The Britisher turned and stared at them icily. "I jolly well shan't run," he replied. "Why should I? I'm perfectly willing to buy you chaps another ball."

The two umpires had taken a terrible riding all through the first game of a double-header. Almost every decision had met with a storm of cat-calls.

When the second game was about to begin, the umpires seemed to have vanished. But a quick check found them seated in the grandstand.

"What goes, you guys?" demanded a group of fans around them. "Ain't you going to umpire this game?"

"Of course we are," said the umps, "but we'll call 'em from here. Seems like you folks can see much better from the stands than we can from out on the field."

The score was tied up in the last half of the fifteenth. Darkness began to envelop the field. The pitcher was in a tight spot. There were two down, but three men were on, and the big hitter was up.

The nervous pitcher motioned to the catcher to meet him for a conference. "Looky here, Butch," he said. "It's so dark now you can hardly see the ball. Still, with this guy, I don't want to take any chances. So I'll wind up and make my pitch—but I won't let go of the ball. Then you smack your fist into the mitt, as if you've caught a perfect strike. Maybe we can fool the ump and have him call it a strike."

The catcher agreed and went back to the plate. But meantime, the home team manager had called the batter over and held a whispered conversation with him.

The umpire called time in, and the batter stepped into his box. The pitcher stepped to the rubber, wound up, and brought his arm down with a snap.

The batsman swung, and over the field there rang the sharp crack of ash meeting horsehide. No one saw the home team manager drop the bat. The batter smiled, looked toward the distant fence, and began trotting around the bases to score a home run.

As four runners came trotting across the plate, the pitcher couldn't say a word. If he admitted he had held on to the ball, the man on third would have scored anyway—on a balk!

The manager, highly indignant over a decision called against his team, strode toward the umpire, his face livid with rage. As he came within a few steps of the umpire, that official yelled, "Get off the field! I'm putting you out of the game."

The manager's jaw dropped. "Why?" he asked. "I ain't even said a word yet."

"No difference," said the umpire. "I know what you're thinking!"

A big, swaggering tough came up to the plate. He scowled at the frail meek-looking umpire behind the plate. Then he turned and faced the pitcher.

The first delivery smacked into the catcher's mitt. "Str-ike one!' called the umpire.

The batter turned and glared menacingly at the man in blue.

Again the pitcher wound up, and once again split the plate with a perfect strike. "Two," yelped the umpire.

"Two what?" roared the yegg, advancing on the arbiter.

"Too low," quaked the ump. "Too low to be a strike."

"Pop," asked the little boy, "what becomes of a ballplayer when his eyesight begins to fail?"

"When that happens, son, they make him an umpire."

One day the devil called up Saint Peter and challenged him to a baseball game.

"Okay," Saint Peter said, "but you know we have all the great players up here."

"Still," the devil said, "you're going to lose."

"Don't be foolish," Saint Peter replied, "we're sure to win. Why, we have Christy Mathewson and Babe Ruth and Ty Cobb and . . ."

"I know," the devil interrupted, "but we have all the umpires down here."

The big league scout telephoned the club manager.

"Joe," he said excitedly, "I just saw a marvelous pitching prospect. This young fellow pitched a no-hitter today. He struck out every single batter he faced. In fact, nobody even hit a foul off him until there were two out in the ninth inning!"

"Sounds good," the manager replied, "but we have enough pitchers right now. What we need is hitters. Sign up the fellow who hit the foul."

One fine morning, a horse walked into a major league ball park and asked the manager for a tryout. When the manager finally recovered from his surprise, he gave the horse a bat, sent him to the plate, and let him try to hit a few pitches. To his amazement, the horse hit each of the first nine pitches into the stands!

"Pretty good," said the manager. "Can you pitch, too?"

"Don't be ridiculous!" said the horse. "Did you ever hear of a horse who could pitch baseball?"

An outfielder, after his playing days were over, became an umpire. The very first time he worked behind the plate—on the very first pitch—the batter gave him an argument.

"That sure looked like a ball to me," the batter said.

"And it would have looked like a ball to me also, *last year,*" the umpire replied, "but from where I'm standing now, it was a strike."

"The Dodgers just lost a game and you sit there calmly knitting!"

"Two with plenty of mustard, Mac!"

"Any message you want sent to your pals on first, second, and third base] I'll be glad to deliver them on my way past!"

"Well, they've finally heard you —they're taking out the pitcher!"

"Now don't try for a home
run, dear. Just bunt me!"

"Junior, why don't you go out and
play baseball with the other boys]"